THE
PEAK
PERFORMANCE
FORMULA

THE
PEAK PERFORMANCE FORMULA

Achieving Breakthrough Results in Life and Work

BY BOB LESSER

THE
collective.
BOOK STUDIO

ISBN: 978-1-951412-20-3

Ebook ISBN: 978-1-951412-25-8

LCCN: 2020915639

Manufactured in the United States of America.

Design by Maureen Forys, Happenstance Type-O-Rama

10 9 8 7 6 5 4 3 2 1

The Collective Book Studio

Oakland, California

This book is dedicated to all the bodhisattvas (parents, teachers, coaches, therapists, leaders, healers, and others) committing their lives to helping others reach their fullest potential. And to my children Satya, Sequoia, and Mischa for giving me the most special of purposes.

CONTENTS

FOREWORD

My initial introduction to Bob came through Jordan Barowitz, my friend from New York's City Hall during Mike Bloomberg's mayoralty. "Hey, there's this guy named Bob Lesser. He runs a charter school in the Bronx. He keeps trying to get me to join their board and I figure I can get out of it if I raise money for them instead. Can you help?" I had just started my first business. Flush with disposable income for the first time in my life, and as someone who believed deeply in education reform, I said yes.

Of course, in fundraising, no good deed goes unpunished. The prize for winning the pie-eating contest is more pie, which meant I soon found myself touring the Mott Hall Charter School, seeing Bob's work in action. I'd been to plenty of charter schools before, so I wasn't surprised by all of the normal signs of a well-run, high-functioning organization. But what struck me were the people who worked there, from the principal to the teachers, administrators, custodians, and everyone else (and Bob made a point of introducing me to all of them). They were so bought in—bought in to the Mott Hall mission, bought in to the Mott Hall culture, bought in to supporting and rooting for one another. It was unusual.

When Bob moved across the country and became an executive coach, it occurred to me that whatever special sauce he developed at Mott Hall probably had utility in other contexts, too. So when one of my partners in our venture capital fund asked if I knew any good coaches,

I sent him Bob's way. Four years later, our venture team had become perhaps the most productive and cohesive in our entire organization (which ranges from the fund to a political consulting firm to a family foundation trying to bring about mobile voting in the United States to a casino management company, a telereligion start-up, media outlets like a podcast, a column for Fast Company, a memoir, a novel and, soon, a bookstore and public podcast studio—our work can get pretty complicated, pretty fast).

Over time, other senior managers on my team have worked with Bob, too, each swearing up and down that they've become better leaders, better listeners, and better partners than ever. It's unfortunate that not everyone can work with Bob one-on-one to learn how to become better leaders, but anyone can read this book.

Understanding your purpose, your values, your vision is something we all can figure out with enough information, the right direction, and a lot of hard work. Learning how to perform at your highest level is not something that requires a degree in psychology or a stint playing in the NBA. It means asking yourself hard questions, being honest about the answers, seeing where you need to improve and what you need to do differently, and then putting the work in to make it happen, day in, day out. This book offers a road map to do just that.

When Bob asked me to write the foreword to his book, it was a testimonial I was eager to provide. I've seen a lot of talented people in my life learn firsthand from Bob's wisdom, his ideas, his intellectual framework. I've seen the ways it's helped their clarity, their confidence, their composure. And knowing that, it can only be good for society to see even more people benefit from Bob's wisdom, too.

BRADLEY TUSK
Founder and CEO of Tusk Ventures

INTRODUCTION

Ow can you achieve and sustain performance at your highest level? We all hit walls in our life pursuits: personal, career, athletic, and others. And when we do, we need new ways to break through and move forward. This book will give you the keys to peak performance and show you how, when applied, they will supercharge individual, team, and organizational outcomes. This book is for anyone who wants to reach new and sustained levels of performance. In short, I'm going to show you how to be a peak performer. By peak performer, I don't necessarily mean being THE best, but rather being YOUR best by consistently meeting the goals you set for yourself based on your vision of how you see yourself. You can apply this to getting your grades up in school, to nailing your first job out of college, to becoming a better parent or athlete, to making the leap into a management role in your organization, to founding your own company.

I draw from research in the fields of psychology, neuroscience, and business. Moreover, I draw from my own experience as a psychotherapist and a former founder and CEO, as well as from my current role as an executive coach working with high-performing leaders. Because learning from experts is a key way to improve performance, I include interviews with peak performers from across multiple disciplines. The interviews operate on two levels. First, I identify the skills and tactics these folks use to generate high levels of performance. These interviews helped validate the research, best practices, and my own experience.

Second, and just as important, they show that by consistently surrounding yourself with people who are performing at the levels you seek to reach you begin to see yourself belonging in that group—like "hey, that could be me." So I literally reached out to my network and asked them to put me in touch with people who performed at extremely high levels with passion and purpose. We all have a network of people who have mastered aspects of what we are seeking to improve upon. I'm excited to share mine with you. But first, let me begin by telling you a story about a boy and a little mouse.

My journey started when I was in elementary school and read a book called *Stuart Little* for a report assignment. It was about a little mouse who is adopted by a family in New York City (where I was born and raised). Despite being so small he finds ways to fit in and be helpful. I loved the book so much that I wrote a fourteen-page book report. I even decorated my own cover. When I got it back from the teacher, expecting to be praised for my passion and effort, the teacher's note simply said that the report was too long. That was the first of many occasions where those responsible for my growth and development wouldn't honor my potential. But like Stuart, I was all about finding ways to outperform what was expected of me.

Years later, as a young working adult trying to figure out what I wanted to be when I grew up, I faced a common dilemma—should I choose to pursue a career offering stability and a good income or follow my passion and hopefully turn it into a successful career? Through a string of jobs and career choices that attempted to navigate this dilemma I would come to find out that the decision was not so simple. The foundations to a successful life were much more nuanced. And after mostly following my interests without much thought about where it was all going, things came to a head.

In the fall of 2012, I founded a charter school to serve low-income families in the South Bronx. I was inspired to open Mott Hall Charter School by my passion for social justice and my belief that education can indeed be a great equalizer.

I was a little apprehensive. But I was also confident. I had graduated from Harvard's Kennedy School of Government, where I studied leadership and management theory, and was trained in conflict resolution. I'd been chief of staff for the New York City Police Department Office of Community Affairs, where I helped rebuild police-community relations in post-September 11th New York City. I'd been associate director of the Office of New Schools at the New York City Department of Education, working at the epicenter of the nation's largest and most ambitious school-reform effort. And to top it off, I'd spent years mastering my mind and emotions, studying mindfulness meditation with Zen masters in Vietnam. Surely, all of this experience would make me the ideal person to open a nice middle school in the South Bronx where poor kids could get a good education.

Although I'd received an excellent education and had been in leadership positions, the school was the first time I would be "The Leader." As prepared as I thought I was, in the process I would get my ass kicked. On the first day of school, the nearby streets were closed, cordoned off because of a "hostage and homicide" incident that happened the night before at the bodega across the street. The number one topic of conversation among the students was the gunshots they heard from their bedrooms. In the weeks and years that followed, there were regular gang fights, drug deals, and murders in the vicinity of our school. The neighborhood delivered a continual dose of what's known in the trauma field as "chronic stress."

Our school families lived with the stresses day in and day out. But I didn't. After each school day, I would leave the neighborhood and go home. Still, I couldn't escape the effects of working in the environment, and I felt guilty for not being stronger. I was also worn down by the hours-long daily commute via subway and bus (if you've never taken a bus in the Bronx, it can be a harrowing ride). And I carried the stress of running an organization as complex as a school where kids' life chances were at stake. We dealt with angry and occasionally violent parents. We expelled kids for bringing weapons to school. We hired good teachers and fired bad teachers and faced constant pressure to exceed state test scores.

Many days I felt under siege, alone, with no one to confide in and no end in sight. My wife, who of course wanted the best for me and our family, would tell me that I needed to resign. I'd gotten the school up and running, she'd say, and that was enough. We had a young daughter whom I didn't see enough of. I was out of the house before she woke up and back home when it was time for her to go to bed. On weekends, I either had to work or I was too exhausted to give my full energy at home. I knew my wife was right, but I plowed on, committed to the work and my desire to succeed. "One more year," I would tell her and myself. "I need one more year to get it right." But the year would come and go, and there was still more to do.

I drove myself to physical and emotional exhaustion. Once every few months, I would crash physically, arriving home from a particularly tough day with a splitting headache, passing out, and forcing myself to get up the next morning and do it all again. The job was draining me.

I finally came to my senses and left in 2017. I hired an amazing replacement, consulted with the school's leadership team, and made the decision to remain active with the board of trustees as I took a time-out from the day-to-day intensity of running the school. While I focused my efforts on feeling great again, I also made a promise to myself that I would remain committed to making an impact that was consistent with my purpose and values.

That Bronx school I helped start is still there, continuing to educate the area kids. And I've continued my own career as an executive and organizational coach, empowering others—particularly start-up founders—to become their best selves and build meaningful, successful organizations. Of course, part of me is still in the Bronx. But my experience there taught me an invaluable lesson: *Although passion is vital to any meaningful endeavor, passion alone is not enough to reach your highest potential.* In order to truly excel, we also need three key peak performance ingredients: purpose, values, and vision.

In my time at the school, I knew I was lacking something, because the work was depleting, not energizing. Instead of bringing me joy and fulfillment, it was making me tired and anxious. It wasn't until I started working as an executive coach—and reading all the books I didn't have time to read when I was in the hot seat—that I discovered how important these elements were. These three key components became part of the Peak Performance Formula I developed. Our purpose needs to be clear, we need to be living in alignment with our values, and we need a clear vision of where we want to go. If those three variables are not aligned, things will be much harder than they need to be, and we won't be as successful.

• • •

As I started to look more deeply at what was most meaningful and exciting to me about the work I had done (i.e., my purpose), I realized that what thrilled me the most were the unique challenges and dynamics of a start-up. As a trained executive and leadership coach, I work primarily with founders, helping them develop their leadership skills and, in turn, their organizations. I have the distinct pleasure of being around some of the brightest minds and most exciting ideas in the world. Which brings me, at last, to my purpose: *to be my best, so that I can bring out the best in others.* As long as I'm engaging in work that's about helping others reach their potential and, in the process, enables me to reach mine, I am on-purpose, doing the work I am supposed to be doing.

Articulating that simple purpose statement was no easy task, however. To get my head around the whole concept of purpose I looked to people who seemed to be living purpose-driven and values-aligned lives with a clear vision for what they wanted to achieve. I think you'll agree that such people are fairly unusual. I read everything I could about how they have been able to be so extraordinary. I looked to the fields of neuroscience, psychology, religion, and education for insights. I conducted surveys and interviewed exemplars of clear-purpose individuals who would talk with me. One of my interviewees, a former world-number-one tennis player, I met in a supermarket, where I summoned the courage to approach him, explained what I was working on, and asked him for an interview.

In this book, I'll examine the Peak Performance Formula and provide insights into the following questions:

1. What exactly is purpose and how can you pinpoint yours?

2. How can values improve your fulfillment and performance?

3. How can you utilize vision to ensure you're getting where you want to go, regardless of your chosen endeavor?

Part I of the book introduces you to the Peak Performance Formula, the simple-but-powerful equation to improve performance in any area of your life. We'll take a close look at the key components of purpose (what it is and why it's so important), values (the role they play in self-improvement and success), and vision (the power of creating one and the goal-setting techniques that follow).

In Part II, we'll focus on how to apply the formula to achieve your individual potential. You'll learn tools and techniques used by top performers to maximize themselves. Further, you'll see how to apply the formula to arguably the most important parts of our lives—our families, teams, and organizations.

At the end of each chapter are exercises and activities that will help you apply the concepts, tools, and techniques just presented to your own life and areas of performance focus. And at the end of the book, after I've given you everything you need to make meaningful breakthroughs, you'll find a 30-day challenge, which will provide structured action and accountability to making the changes you are working on stick.

This work is not easy. Performance breakthroughs do not come overnight. Rather, applying the formula is a process of continual doing, reflecting, and learning. Parts of this book will take time to sink in and work for you. And depending on what is happening in your life, some chapters may be more relevant than others. I encourage you to keep coming back to the lessons in these pages when you do hit a wall or feel stuck. I know it's hard to remember in those moments, but setbacks are truly the best opportunities for learning and growth. And we all need help to move past our current limitations.

Drawing on my experience from the front lines of leadership in public, private, and nonprofit organizations, working in big bureaucracies and with cutting-edge venture-backed start-ups, conducting many interviews with top performers from various fields, and working as a therapist and executive coach, I have seen that you can have your cake and eat it too. You can be successful and be happy, you can work hard and be healthy, you can make an impact on the world and with your loved ones. And with the concepts, tools, and techniques in this book I'll show you how.

I know now what I didn't know back in the Bronx: that there are healthy, effective, and sustainable ways to do the incredibly hard work that matters most while striving to reach the highest levels of one's potential. This book shares those methods. When passion aligns with purpose, values, and vision, what results is a powerful, focused, and joyful experience of performance. With this alignment, there is no stopping you.

PART I

The Peak Performance Formula

CHAPTER ONE

The Performance Paradox and the Pillars of Peak Performance

THE PERFORMANCE PARADOX: WHEREVER YOU GO, THERE YOU ARE

While there is a relatively clear path to achieving breakthrough performance, most of us struggle to consistently and sustainably be our best. We know what we should be doing to be our best, but we don't do it. We are our own worst enemies when it comes to achieving our goals. If we are born with limitless potential, what makes it so hard to live up to that potential? For the past twenty years I have been trying to gain some insights into this question through my training in meditation, psychotherapy, and neuroscience. Here's what I've discovered about why it's not so easy to cultivate the focus and endure the hardship required to continually get better. Essentially we are designed to work against ourselves. Here's how:

1. **The Unconscious Mind**

   It is estimated that 95 percent of what happens in our mind is unconscious and therefore out of our awareness. Furthermore, experts estimate that our basic operating principles (understanding of the world, core beliefs about ourselves) are formed by the time we are five years old. So, you've basically got a five-year-old in charge of you. How does this affect us as adults?

   If unresolved, the impact of attachment failures from these early days shows up throughout our lives and can manifest as chronically feeling alone in life, having limiting beliefs about ourselves, or feeling that the world is a negative or unsafe place.

   These early days are also when our egos get conditioned to believe we have worth only around *doing* rather than *being*; we are hurt if and when our potential is not honored; we develop a fear of insignificance, maybe feeling we have to be productive every minute of the day; we develop feelings of entitlement, thinking something we have to do is below us; or we just want to relax and be taken care of, but actually have responsibilities that require us to get off our butts.

   So this is our basic operating system. While you are reading this, it is running you without your awareness or consent. How well are you going to do if you believe you are unworthy of love or success?

2. **The Self-Conscious Mind**

   We yearn to be unique (especially us Americans), to stand out in a crowd. And we are deeply social beings. These traits lead us to develop our sense of self, connect us to our community, and help us empathize with what others are experiencing. They also drive the need we have for meaning and validation, and the aspirations we have that do not always get fulfilled. We have in-groups and out-groups, and form beliefs and prejudices based on identity and group affiliation. In contrast, animals have one goal: survival—to find food and water, and make it through the day. Unlike animals, we as humans care (too much) about what others think of us and spend considerable time and energy trying to be accepted. The needs to be special and for everything to be meaningful, and the desire to achieve and to be accepted, present an extremely tall order. They set us up for inevitable failure, rejection, and pain. Often we would rather not try than to experience these things. It is hard for us to just focus on being better than we were yesterday and to not compare ourselves to others.

3. Our Biology

Our nervous systems have remained relatively unchanged throughout the past few thousands of years of evolution. We have a hardwired stress response system, which prepares us to fight, flee, or freeze. Brain scans show that the same regions of the brain are activated when we experience social pain (e.g., failure, rejection, embarrassment, etc.) as when we experience physical pain. We all have a threshold that psychologists call our "window of tolerance," which, once exceeded, activates our stress response and causes our amygdalas to take over (the part of the brain that controls emotions). In other words, rational thought goes out the window. And because of our ability as humans to think, we can and do ruminate and hold on to stressful events as opposed to just letting them go like animals in the wild. (For a deep dive into this subject, read *Why Zebras Don't Get Ulcers*, by Robert Sapolsky.) We worry about things as trivial as whether our behinds look fat in our jeans or as existential as our deaths.

This constant worry and chronic stress can shrink our window of tolerance. In turn, that causes us to be in an almost constant state of stress response that, over time, has serious emotional and physical consequences.

4. The Hedonic Treadmill

We get bored and antsy easily, and are attracted to new shiny things. When we get these new things, they satisfy us for a while, but then the excitement wears off and dissatisfaction follows, and we chase the next new thing. The psychologist Barry Schwartz calls this unending process the "hedonic treadmill." The mind, untamed, will jump from thought to thought, like a monkey swinging from branch to branch. We do not by nature have a quiet and peaceful mind. This is what psychologists call associative thought and meditators call "monkey mind." The constant distractions generated by our own minds and the attraction to the next shiny object make it hard for us to keep the sustained focus required for continued practice and performance.

5. Our Negativity Hardwiring

To add to all the above, humans have what neuroscientists have dubbed a negativity bias. Our brains are actually wired to focus more on bad things than on good things. Again, this is a relic of our survival imperative, where it was more important for us to see the snake in the woods than the beautiful flower.

The struggle to be our best comes from the way our minds work. Without compensating for this and reconditioning our minds, we will continue to underperform. But if we do the work of getting to know our mind—how it works—and retraining it, we can get out of our own way. We have the means to become the best version of ourselves. That's where the Peak Performance Formula comes in.

THE PILLARS OF PEAK PERFORMANCE

If you don't read another page in this book beyond this short section, you'll be missing out on some really cool stuff. But you'll also have the essence of what you need to attain your peak performance in any endeavor you choose. Through studying peak performance and interviewing scores of high performers from across disciplines from sports to music to politics to business, I have distilled peak performance down to its three most important variables, which I call the Peak Performance Formula:

Purpose + Values + Vision = Peak Performance

Let's take a quick look at each part of the formula to understand what each component is and what this book has in store to help you put the formula into action for yourself. While these components may sound straightforward, they are nuanced and can be slippery to actually apply. I have been refining my understanding of these concepts for years, and only in the past few have they become clear to the point that I can convey them to you.

Purpose

Chapter Two of the book defines purpose—what it is and why it is a key component for performance. Purpose drives motivation, and the more motivation we have the more energy, resilience, and perseverance we have to get things done. Purpose gives what we do meaning. And as human beings we crave meaning in some ways more than anything. The interviews with on-purpose individuals quickly show how important purpose is in driving one's success. The chapter ends with some exercises on how to clarify your own purpose. If life is like being in a rowboat at sea, purpose is the North Star that gives us guidance and direction in the dark of night.

Values

Next, we examine the second key building block of self-improvement and success—values. Chapter Three provides a definition for values, delves into why they are so important, and introduces the powerful concept of values alignment. The chapter provides activities to help you determine what's most important to you, how much you're currently living those things, where the gaps exist, and how to bring more values alignment to your life. Values are the oars that we use to propel ourselves toward where we want to go.

Vision

It is so important to have a clear and compelling picture of where you are going—to have a vision. The more detailed and nuanced the picture, the more compelling it will be and the more likely you are to get there. Chapter Four shares the power and process of creating vision and the goal-setting that follows. Vision is the destination where we want to arrive.

Once you understand the nuances of the Peak Performance Formula, we offer tools, techniques, and real-life applications to help you implement these principles in your life, in your family, for the teams you lead, and the organizations you run. By putting this formula into practice you cannot help but get better.

CHAPTER TWO

Purpose—
The First Peak
Performance Pillar

P urpose has been understood and utilized in religion for centuries to catalyze devotion (anyone who follows a call to serve god is demonstrating a religious-driven purpose), but its application to improving performance and fulfillment is a more recent phenomenon. This chapter elaborates on how purpose is a key variable in the performance formula, what it is, and how it works. Most important, it provides guidance to help you hone your unique purpose in life.

BRENT BAKER, FOUNDER AND CEO, TRI-STATE BIO DIESEL

How purpose makes everything else possible

Brent Baker is an environmental activist and the founder of Tri-State Biodiesel, a company whose mission is to provide cleaner-burning biodiesel fuel as an alternative to gasoline. The day I visited Brent's office seemed like it was one of those frustrating days in the life of a start-up. It was well past 5 p.m., yet everyone was still in the office. The team was trying to problem-solve delivery trucks breaking down, an injured driver, possible fuel contamination, and the possibility of having to cancel deliveries.

Before becoming an entrepreneur, Brent was a longtime environmental activist. During his later years in high school, he organized traveling circuses to provide people with information on sustainability. As he continued to learn about sustainability Brent was inspired to do more. He became interested in natural home building and took classes, attended workshops, and worked on homes in different parts of the country. During the year, Brent would work as a carpenter to support himself and then spend the summer traveling around the country to promote sustainability.

When I asked him why the environment and not something else like poverty, war, hunger, or any of the many worthy causes out there he said, "The environment, and especially global warming, affects everyone and needs to be addressed. The preservation of our planet should be our number one priority, and everything else should come second."

Brent first became hooked on biodiesel when two environmental activists who called themselves the Veggie Babes drove cross-country completely on biodiesel fuel. "I fell in love immediately! Petroleum is one of the most detrimental products to the environment. With biodiesel, we can grow our own fuel, reduce carbon emissions, and become less dependent on oil." Brent got even more excited with the discovery that you can fuel vehicles on ordinary restaurant oil without any additional chemicals. "I realized that if biodiesel was going to have any real impact on the environment that it had to become a mass consumer product."

For a couple of hundred dollars over the Internet, Brent incorporated a new company that would produce and distribute biodiesel fuel. But although he had experience running a nonprofit and writing grant proposals, Brent was a fish out of water in the business world. He had to figure out how to write a business plan and how to raise serious investment dollars. He started researching and talking to people, and because he was known for his environmental activism it didn't take long before he was able to attract interest and help from people who knew how to develop businesses and had money. He learned finance and accounting, figured out how to read contracts, talked to people in the field. And after about eight months, he had a business plan that was good enough to attract an angel investor who would help the company launch.

Brent tells me how important it is to believe in yourself, your abilities, and your purpose. "At first no one would take us seriously and everything took longer than we expected. The bankers, lawyers, and insurance companies wouldn't give us the time of day initially. I didn't know if we could succeed, but I knew that I needed determination and stamina." Brent recalls many long hours and sleepless nights with the company on the brink of disaster. "Setbacks have been the norm. You have to look at these things as opportunities for learning. Otherwise it would be too easy to bail out and say this isn't doable. I try to stay calm, keep perspective on why I'm doing this, and remember our successes. When things get really bad I think, 'If I don't fight for this, I can't expect anyone else to.'"

What Brent and his partners are doing is pretty phenomenal. They are creating a new industry that has not existed before. "There are a lot of resources and capital out there for green projects that make sense," Brent advises. He encourages anyone whose purpose is fighting climate change to go for it. Purpose is what allowed Brent to create something from nothing, even when no one else thought what he was doing would work. It helped him keep going, despite encountering setback after setback. His sense of purpose is what makes everything else possible.

"WHAT'S YOUR PURPOSE?"

One of the most popular courses at Harvard's Kennedy School of Government is on adaptive leadership, which is a methodology for leading through challenges that do not have ready-made answers. In my class students spent a good part of the semester being asked the question, "What's your purpose?" Like most of my classmates, I stumbled through and had great difficulty coming up with an answer. According to Professor Ron Heifetz, the creator of the course and this approach to leadership, purpose is what gives you clarity and courage to act in difficult situations that do not have clear answers. While the class posed the question, it didn't offer much guidance in how to actually answer it. For that I would need about twenty more years of struggling with this question, reading what was out there on the subject, and applying trial and error with approaches that would lead to an answer. In a recent conversation, Dr. Heifetz reassured me that just pondering the question has value. And he explained, purpose is so important because it helps clarify what really matters and points us to what we should be using our skills and talents for. *By embodying our purpose, expressing it through words, pictures, music, or other means we can deploy it to help solve the problems we care most about.*

So why is articulating our purpose so hard? First of all, what is purpose exactly? Without a definition it's hard to even know where to start.

Defining Your Personal Purpose

At its most basic I define purpose as "the expression of what's most deeply meaningful to you, who you are at your essence." Getting to one's deepest essence is tough, though. As we're growing up, we aren't given space to think about who we are at essence, and then as adults most of us are too preoccupied leading our busy lives full of obligations and responsibilities to ponder such a question. Brent Baker, the founder and CEO of Tri-State Biodiesel, had strong conviction that his purpose, the most important thing to him, involved preserving the planet. This made it easier for him to narrow down and pursue the ideas that would most fit his purpose. Not all of us have that level of conviction or clarity. The distinctions offered below can help you define it more quickly.

... IS NOT A TITLE OR ROLE

When we do start to try to get to these deeper layers of who we are we often get stuck at the more surface elements of ourselves. We tend to overidentify with our jobs or roles, for instance. We say things like "I am a CEO" or "I am a parent" rather than being able to describe the core of who we are. It's like an onion where we have to peel back layers to get to the center. So if we are not our job or our role in life than what the heck are we?

... IS ALWAYS TRUE

Your purpose has to apply universally to your life and be true no matter the time and place. It has to be general enough to always be true but specific enough that it actually means something to you and can provide clear guidance and direction to your actions. While it's relatively easy to come up with a statement of purpose that holds true for one situation, it can be hard to create something that is always true. But it has to be, since it's who you are at your essence, and that doesn't change depending on the situation. When we are at our best we are expressing our purpose in everything we do.

... IS ABOUT IMPACT

Purpose is about the essence of who we are, and the impact we have on others and the world as an expression of that essence. Purpose is something we must bring to the world. And our sense of purpose is enhanced when we do so. In one study, sixth graders recounted that projects that impacted others were the activities that made them feel the most proud, successful, and creative. They gave examples of such activities as tutoring younger children, learning to make public presentations, designing blueprints for playhouses that would actually be built and donated to preschools. Even from a young age we want to engage in activities we know will have impact.

... PROVIDES GUIDANCE AND DIRECTION

Purpose is like a compass or the North Star. It provides us with direction and guidance on what we should be doing; shows us how we should be spending our time; and gives us inspiration, courage, and clarity to move toward action and in every situation. It's about action.

... STRETCHES US

In order for things to be motivating to us, challenges must stretch us enough so that they remain motivating. Activities that are too easy quickly lose their novelty and become boring. Activities that are too difficult overload and frustrate us. Being on-purpose involves stretching ourselves enough so that what we are doing is challenging but not impossible.

Now that we have the basics down, let's take a deeper dive into the mechanics of purpose.

How Does Something Become Meaningful to Us?

Going back to our definition above, purpose is about meaning and what we care most deeply about. There is no "right" purpose. Different people have different purposes, depending on what is uniquely meaningful to each of us. As human beings, how do we come to care about things and assign meaning to some things over and above others? Understanding this will help us get to the more elusive core of what matters most to us.

Excitement and Reward

It all starts with excitement and reward. These are two of the most powerful drivers of what motivates people. The more stimulating an activity and the bigger the potential payoff, the more likely we are to feel motivated to pursue it. Novelty and reward are two primary stimuli that direct us to focus attention and exert energy. The brain's novelty function identifies new stimuli and the reward function produces sensations of pleasure.

Arousal, motor orientation, novelty, reward, and organization comprise the brain's attention system. Incoming information from our external environment or our thoughts can get us excited, depending on the attention value of that stimulus. The amygdala (an almond-shaped region of the mid-brain) assigns emotional significance to incoming information on a scale of mildly interesting to high alert. If it rates high enough, our arousal apparatus is alerted. The hippocampus, which is a critical player in long-term memory, allows us to compare the present with the past to determine if what is happening is meaningful or not. If we're getting overly excited about something mundane, our memory tells us and our hippocampus calms things down to conserve the brain's energy. But if our hippocampus signals that what's happening is meaningful, off we go, motivation and purpose turned on.

In the 1950s, the psychologist James Olds demonstrated that animals will work extremely hard in order to experience stimulation of the pleasure centers of the brain. In his experiments, lab rats quickly learned to switch on electrodes that stimulated parts of their brains that resulted in pleasure, and they continued to activate these electrodes to the point of exhaustion. They almost totally ignored other needs such as food, water, sex, and sleep. Repeat—they ignored food, water, sex, and sleep for this pleasure associated with reward. The animals would continue to provide rewards for themselves for long periods of time, occasionally taking a break only to get something to eat before returning to reward stimulation.

The novelty and reward systems provide the arousal and energy that make us interested in the world around us. They get us excited and generate a feeling that something good will happen if we explore the environment or engage with objects. More often than not, our novelty and reward systems are being fully activated when we are in the midst of pursuing what we care about. And at full tilt these activities can be more rewarding than food, water, sex, and sleep.

So the things that are most meaningful to us likely had their origins in something that registered in your brain as new and important, and the reward centers of your brain may have been activated from positive feedback, praise, or adrenaline that made you feel compelled to want more.

Since the Olds experiments where lab rats pursued pleasure over everything else, other pleasure centers of the brain have been identified. These areas guide us to focus our energy and attention on stimuli that will result in reward and pleasure. Locating these areas in the brain was a significant discovery, as was the discovery of what made these pleasure centers work. Neurotransmitters and endorphins (the body's natural opiates) play a key role in feeling reward and pleasure. Dopamine, serotonin, norepinephrine, and endorphins are the body's natural chemicals responsible for creating the feelings of drive, excitement, and reward that incentivize our engagement in meaningful activities. Let's learn a little more about how these work.

DOPAMINE

Parts of the brain that make up the reward system contain high concentrations of the neurotransmitter dopamine. Large amounts of dopamine are released in response to pleasurable rewards. When we accomplish something, our brain triggers the release of dopamine, and we experience a surge of pleasures, energy, and confidence. We learn to associate positive emotions with specific events through the release of dopamine. Dopamine strengthens the prolonged chemical firing of signals and allows for uninterrupted communication between neurons. It decreases random neural firing and also makes the neurons it affects more ready to fire. Dopamine allows us to concentrate longer and harder, and makes neural communication more efficient and effective. Because of this, it has been dubbed the learning neurotransmitter. Dopamine may both help us feel good when we are on-purpose and provide the nudge to stay engaged with our purpose when it gets challenging.

SEROTONIN

Serotonin is also found in high concentrations in regions of the brain that make up the rewards system. Serotonin regulates aggression, mood, sexual activity, sleep, and sensitivity to pain. It calms us, elevates our mood and self-esteem, and prevents the brain from getting out of control from fear and worry. When we find something meaningful and spend time developing our knowledge and skills in that area, serotonin release creates a virtuous cycle for us of feeling good when we do that thing.

NOREPINEPHRINE

Norepinephrine, also known as noradrenaline, plays a large role in arousal, attention, and focus. This neurotransmitter is activated by a stressful (not necessarily in a bad way) event and is related to the body's fight or flight readiness response. Its release increases the heart rate and blood pressure, opens up air passages to the lungs, and readies the skeletal muscles for action. We all know the term "adrenaline junky" and, while that might not describe us, chances are that when we are on-purpose it engages our levels of arousal, attention, and focus thanks to norepinephrine.

ENDORPHINS

Endorphins (meaning endogenous morphine) are the body's natural pain killers. They are peptides, tiny pieces of proteins, which resemble opiates like morphine and opium in their ability to ease pain and produce a sense of peaceful, euphoric bliss. They work by connecting to the opiate receptor cells in the brain. As with norepinephrine, we often engage in activities that will release this peptide. Endorphins are released during long and continuous periods of exercise when the intensity level is between moderate and difficult, and breathing is somewhat difficult. Some experts believe that just completing a challenge, whether it's physically taxing or not, is accompanied by an endorphin release. When we are doing something that is intensely aligned with our purpose there may be some endorphin release.

The brain's mechanisms for motivation, excitement, and reward play a key role in how we assign meaning to things in our lives, and neurochemicals such as dopamine, serotonin, norepinephrine, and endorphins play a key role in this process as well. Purpose usually comes about through intense experiences (good or bad) that get labeled as important to us, and then we seek to engage in these experiences again and again.

SURVIVAL OF THE FITTEST (BRAIN CELLS, THAT IS)

Through a process called Neural Darwinism, groups of neurons compete with each other to survive in the brain. Frequently used neural groups thrive and develop strong interconnections while those that are not used weaken or die. The more importance we attach to an activity, the more neurons are made available for that activity. When we are born, our brain learns by mere exposure to the world since our learning machinery, the nucleus basalis, is continuously on, producing acetylcholine, which allows us to focus our attention. In adulthood, this is not the case. The nucleus basalis is only turned on when something important, surprising, or novel occurs or if we make an effort to pay close attention. When our attention is divided, as is the case when we try to multitask, our learning machinery stays off and we don't retain much. But when we make explicit and prioritize the things we most care about and do them without distraction, we are literally driving neurons to those activities. With repeated effort, those neural connections become both stronger and more automatic. With enough focus, because paying close attention is essential to creating permanent change in our brains, and with enough practice, we can move ourselves from going through the motions to feeling fully on-purpose more of the time. And thanks to an excellent design feature in our brains known as neuroplasticity, which is our ability to form new neural connections at any age, we can keep growing and get better throughout life.

SOURCES OF PURPOSE

Now that we understand how meaning gets assigned to things in our lives, let's turn to some of the more common categories and sources of purpose, the things that most often touch us at the deepest places in our hearts.

THE WILL TO SURVIVE

(Case Study: Ethan Zohn)

Ethan Zohn is a survivor. Literally. He won the reality show *Survivor: Africa* and later beat cancer. His purpose and core values were essential in helping him accomplish both.

Ethan's father passed away when Ethan was fourteen years old. When that happened, the entire community came out to embrace him, and he learned the power of support. That experience gave him the confidence and courage to say yes to new experiences. As a kid, Ethan had dreams of becoming a professional athlete. He played soccer growing up and in college, and after showing up to an open tryout he made the cut to play professional soccer. "Once I realized there was potential to play professionally is when I kicked things into high gear," Ethan recounted in our conversation. "If I'm going to do this, I'm going to dig in and work hard." He accomplished this through a regimen of workouts and training to get in shape, enlisting a coach to master the technical side and a sports psychologist who taught him mental skills, including visualization and meditation.

And the work paid off. Ethan played professional soccer in Hawaii, Israel, and for the Zimbabwe Premier League. "My strongest memory from my time in Zimbabwe was when the team traveled to away games and I'd see these graveyards along the side of the road. Some were very nicely organized while others were hastily piled up. I came to learn that the scattered areas were where people who died from AIDS were buried. To see a physical representation of the disease and the stigma associated with dying from it was striking. And it really stuck in my head."

Then in 2002 Ethan set out for a new adventure, being a contestant on the reality TV show *Survivor.* The show in its third season would bring him back to Africa to compete against fifteen other contestants for $1 million. "*Survivor* is designed to push every part of you—physical, emotional, mental, and spiritual—to the limit, and then to push you some more." So how do you step up to a challenge like this?

The goal of *Survivor* is to be the last person standing. As players get voted out, they become the ones who come back to decide who wins. "You have to have a strategy going in, and mine was to be cutthroat," recounts Ethan. But take away food, water, and sleep, and then cut people off from everything that makes them comfortable, and the strategy goes out the window. "I realized I couldn't be someone I wasn't." You have to be authentic, and your purpose and values have to be a true expression of who you are. If they're not, you will be unable to execute.

"So I played the game like I lived my life, with the skill sets that served me well to that point: knowing myself and what I bring to the table, being a crucial and selfless member of the community." This is Ethan's purpose, defined in large part when his father died, and it grounded his decisions and actions throughout the game. "To me, being a crucial member of the community meant getting the water, doing the chores, trying to find food, and building the shelter, so that without me they would struggle. I ended up losing a challenge on purpose and letting someone else win to build trust with him based on my belief that being selfless would pay off in the end."

And pay off it did. Thanks to his guiding values Ethan won the entire thing, the $1 million prize. And he didn't get a single vote against him during the entire game. While on *Survivor* he had the opportunity to play a game of hacky sack with children who were HIV positive. This brought him back to the memory of the graves in Zimbabwe. Later, with the prize money, Ethan cofounded a nonprofit organization called Grassroots Soccer (GS), which uses the power of soccer to inspire and mobilize young people to make healthier life choices. Started in 2003, GS is now in fifty countries and has graduated 2.3 million kids.

The story doesn't end here. Eight years later Ethan was diagnosed with a rare form of blood cancer. He underwent chemo and radiation treatment, and he ultimately needed a bone marrow transplant. "This time I wasn't competing for a million dollars but for my life." Ethan took on cancer using the same set of core values and peak performance techniques he developed playing soccer and winning *Survivor.* "I saw cancer as an opportunity to share my story and help others out there, so I made my recovery public. Through these experiences I've really come to see that helping people helps you heal as a human being."

Using his purpose of service over self and helping others, Ethan's current focus is as a thought leader and advocate in the health and wellness field using medicine derived from nature or that comes from within. When asked what advice he has for people, he offers the following: "Don't worry about failing; worry about all the things you'll miss if you don't even try." Ethan's is a lesson in making sense of life by finding deeper purpose. (You can learn more about Ethan and his work at ethanzohn.com and grassrootssoccer.org.)

FIGHTING FOR A CAUSE

(Case Study: Lhadon Tethong)

For many, purpose is found in a cause that is based on universal ethics such as social justice, freedom, equality, or human rights. Many people have put themselves in harm's way, been hurt, or been killed for their stalwart belief in these principles.

Lhadon Tethong is deeply committed to freedom and justice. When we met, Lhadon was working to empower and train youth as leaders in a worldwide movement for social justice through education, grassroots organizing, and nonviolent direct action. Lhadon's father is Tibetan, and he lived in exile after the Chinese invaded Tibet in 1949. And Lhadon's mom spent twelve years living in India, working with Tibetan refugees. Because of her upbringing. Lhadon's desire to bring about freedom for her people is rooted in her earliest memories. "From as far back as I can remember I was always around hot, passionate discussions of Tibetan issues and going to protests." Her own career as an activist started in the sixth grade when she became interested in animal rights and started a campaign at her school to raise awareness about cruelty to animals. In high school, Lhadon began to teach others about multiculturalism and anti-racism. And in college, she started a local chapter of Students for a Free Tibet.

On more than one occasion, Lhadon has put herself in harm's way in her attempts to raise awareness and gain public attention for human rights in Tibet. During a protest in China in the lead-up to the 2008 Olympic Games, Lhadon was arrested and eventually deported by the Chinese government. "I was extremely scared at the prospects of imprisonment and what could happen to me. But the goal is so strong and so clear that it makes taking risks easier. I wanted to be there face-to-face, and it felt right." Lhadon is sure to point out that there are limits to her fearlessness, but that her belief in her cause helps keep things clear and helps her push the limits.

As Lhadon's example shows, a strong sense of purpose helps one walk the walk. "You have to do what you're asking others to do. Protest, give money, volunteer, get arrested in China. Then you have to inspire in people a belief that change is possible, tell them how, and show them the way." She cautions us to remember that not everyone is going to be as clear and willing to take risks as others might be. "But if you are guided by your heart and show your emotion it will draw other people to you and bring them along."

LOVE AND SERVICE

(Case Study: Dick Hoyt)

Dick Hoyt's son, Rick, was born without the ability to walk or speak. All the experts recommended that Rick be put in an institution where he could be looked after. But the Hoyts could not bear the thought of having their son miss all the experiences of life like any other child. So they raised Rick with the mindset that he could do anything that anyone else could do. With this mindset, Rick asked his father if the two could compete in a five-mile race to benefit a local college athlete who had been paralyzed in a car accident. When I talked to Dick he recounted that "Rick wanted to show that life goes on even if you're paralyzed." In Rick's formfitting Mulholland wheelchair, which Dick pushed while he ran, the two completed the race, finishing second to last. After the race, Rick told his father, "Dad, when we were running, I felt like I wasn't disabled anymore." Dick wanted to give his son this feeling as often as he could. Beginning in 1977 up to the time of my conversation with Dick, the two had completed more than 1,047 endurance events, including sixty-nine marathons and six Ironman triathlons. During the Ironman competitions, Dick swims 2.4 miles with a strap around his waist, pulling an eight-foot dingy with Rick aboard; he then rides 112 miles with Rick in front of the handlebars, sitting in a specially constructed seat on the front tire of his bike; and finally he runs a full-length marathon, pushing Rick in a custom-designed twenty-seven-pound wheelchair. At seventy years old, Dick was still racing almost thirty times per year. "Rick is my motivation," Dick says. "I don't do this for myself, but for Rick, so that he can have the experience. I'm just the body, he's the heart."

What drove Dick to complete more than a thousand endurance events was not his ego; it was his deep sense of love for his son and dedication to give him experiences of a normal life and to inspire people to do the same. The strongest purpose often involves serving others.

Love is one of the most powerful sources of purpose for us. Anyone who has ever been in love with another person knows its power. Because we care so deeply for that person, we will do whatever we can to make his or her life as good as can be. Whether it is caring for a sick partner, working two jobs to earn extra money to support your family, or going to great lengths to plan a party for a friend, doing things for people we love makes us feel good and gives our lives meaning and satisfaction. In his book *Man's Search for Meaning,* the concentration camp survivor and psychiatrist Viktor E. Frankl says, "Love is the ultimate and highest goal to which man can aspire." When he was all but certain he could not survive another day in Auschwitz, his love for his wife, whose status he did not know, kept him going. He writes, "The guard passed by, insulting me, and once again I communed with my beloved. More and more I felt that she was present, that she was with me; I had the feeling that I was able to touch her, able to stretch out my hand and grasp hers. The feeling was very strong: she was there. Then, at that very moment, a bird flew down silently and perched just in front of me, on the heap of soil which I had dug up from the ditch, and looked steadily at me."

People who are able to tap into their feelings of love and can keep that love flowing, as hard as it is in the cynical world we live in, are able to maintain a powerful connection to their life's purpose.

LOSS DRIVES CHANGE

(Case Study: Nancy Baker)

Sometimes our sense of purpose is brought into focus through a loss or other trauma we experience. By helping to make sure others never have to experience that loss or by caring for people who have experienced a similar trauma, our actions help to make meaning out of and in some way heal the wounds of the pain we experienced.

In 2002, Nancy Baker's seven-year-old daughter, Graeme, drowned after becoming trapped by the suction of a spa drain. Still in the fog of grief, Nancy learned that Graeme's death was the result of faulty machinery and could have been prevented. As she did more research, she learned that hundreds of children had died from drain entrapment and that the pool and spa industry had fought previous attempts at regulation.

This infuriated Nancy. And initially, anger is what motivated her to act. An introvert by nature and a painter who preferred solitude, Nancy forced herself to meet with parent and consumer groups to raise awareness about this issue. "I learned everything I never wanted to know about drowning," Nancy recounts. She then began to meet with members of Congress to push for federal legislation that would ensure that no other parent would experience what she had. Officials told her that federal legislation on this issue would never pass, and that while tragic it did not affect enough people.

The haunting memories of being underwater, trying to pull her daughter to safety, quickly overpowered whatever discouragement she felt. She founded an organization called Safe Kids that was interested in helping. And then a junior congresswoman who had heard her story contacted her, because she was interested in championing this issue. "I began to feel like my advocacy was no accident. It was like something so wrong had happened that finally the universe said, 'That's it, enough!'"

Nancy says that the spirit of her daughter has given her incredible motivation to see this through. She appeared on *Larry King Live* and other national news programs to gain support. While she expected to be terrified, she was not. Instead, she found she was so driven by the opportunity to save more kids from dying that she was not nervous at all.

The Virginia Graeme Baker Pool and Spa Safety Act was approved by Congress and signed into law by President George W. Bush on December 19, 2007. What began as a mother's angry search for answers transformed into a deep expression of love for her daughter and a mission to save other children and parents from experiencing this unimaginable pain and loss.

What drove Nancy to overcome her doubts and fears, and into action, was a deeper sense of purpose.

IDENTITY AS A CATALYST

(Case Study: Suraya Sadeed)

In a world that often defines us by our identity—whether it be national, ethnic, religious, racial, gender, sexual orientation, or other—our life experiences around our identity can become an important part of our purpose.

Suraya Sadeed was a happily married mother and successful businesswoman. One day, life as she knew it came crashing

down. Just a day before their daughter's high school gradua-
tion, her husband died of a heart attack. In the midst of her own
pain and loss, Suraya, who was born and raised in Afghanistan,
decided to return home to Kabul. In Afghanistan, she witnessed
hundreds of thousands of people who had lost everything from
the 1998 earthquake and war that began in 2001. "They had no
real future," Suraya recalls, "just painful memories." She remembers one nineteen-year-old girl who was pregnant, already with
two kids, and whose husband and parents had been killed, living
under a plastic tent. "What was amazing was that this girl still
had such determination and hope. It shook me. I returned to the
United States a changed person. I no longer had the drive to
make money. I could keep mourning my own loss or I could do
something to help."

Suraya founded a nonprofit organization called Help the
Afghan Children. "No one knew what Afghanistan was at that
time, they couldn't even pronounce it, so it was hard to raise
funds initially," she recalls. But with persistence she was able to
raise enough money to do something. "The Taliban was incredibly
repressive and brutal, and so much of the oppression in Afghanistan was directed at women and girls. Formal education for girls
was forbidden, and women were regularly beaten. I kept asking,
'Why be punished for being a woman?' So that's where I decided
to start."

Suraya raised $100,000. And with the money literally strapped
to her body, she entered Afghanistan at night through Pakistan.
During the crossing they were stopped and searched by Taliban
soldiers who found music in the car, which under Taliban law was
illegal. "They confiscated the tapes, called us sinners, and told us
we had better pray." After being detained overnight, they were

finally released, and Suraya was able to deliver the money to her local partners to start and support seventeen schools for girls. "There was definitely risk to my life, but I never had a second thought, because the reward was so great. After losing my husband and seeing so much death as a result of the earthquake and war I was less scared of dying."

Suraya often sees the faces of the girls she has helped over the years, and these faces keep her going. "If these girls who have suffered so much still have hope, so should I. Their determination drives me. Every time I make another trip to Afghanistan I say it's my last. But when I get there, it changes me again and I say, 'Maybe one more time.' I feel a satisfaction that never existed in my business life. It's an inner satisfaction that comes from changing people's lives rather than a never-ending quest for more money.

You now have a more thorough understanding of purpose than 99 percent of the population. With this knowledge you are ready to get to work on your own purpose.

YOUR TURN—PURPOSE STATEMENT EXERCISE

Purpose is a hard thing to articulate. Those of us in the peak performance and coaching worlds who have come to understand the power of purpose in helping people get better have invariably struggled for years trying to nail down our own purpose. And for many of us it remains a work in progress. Here are some exercises to help you get to the essence of yours.

Think of two times when you felt most alive, most fulfilled, most impactful. What are they and what do they have in common?

You are starting a nonprofit organization to make an impact on a cause that matters deeply to you. What does the organization do?

You have one post on social media that has been guaranteed to go viral. Millions of people will see it and repost it. What does it say?

What are your superpowers? These are attributes or things you do that come so naturally to you that you may not be able to recognize them without some help. If this is the case ask a few people who know you well. Often the things they reflect back to you hold some clues to your deeper purpose.

Reflect on a saying or motto that captures your purpose. What is it?

Now take a look at all the words and phrases you generated, then circle the ones that feel most important to you. From this list, come up with a draft purpose statement that resonates with you, using the following format. Pulling from the words and phrases above, come up with a phrase that captures the essence of who you are and the impact you want to make as a result. Your purpose should be universally true, meaning it applies to all aspects of your life. It's a first draft, so you can revise it later:

I am _____ (essence of being) who _____ _____ (Impact on the world)

Example: I am my best who makes others their best. Or if I'm feeling more metaphorical, I am the vital spark who fires up potential.

CHAPTER THREE

Values—
The Second Peak
Performance Pillar

I f purpose is the North Star providing the rowboat guidance and direction in the dark night sky, then values are the oars that do the work of rowing us to our destination. This chapter covers the second key building block of performance: values. It provides a definition for values, delves into why they are so important, and introduces the powerful concept of values alignment. Then you'll find activities that will help you determine what's most important to you, how much you're currently living those things, where the gaps exist, and how to bring more values alignment to your life.

MAX ERDSTEIN, GOOGLE EMPLOYEE NUMBER TWENTY-FOUR

When your values tell you to walk away from being king of the world

In 1999, Max Erdstein was getting ready to graduate from Stanford University and was looking for a way to stay close to campus while his girlfriend attended school the following fall. Max's freshman-year roommate, who was one of the founding employees at a small Internet start-up with a funny name, hired him. When he joined, Max was employee twenty-four. The company was Google, and Max's job was to develop their marketing and advertising function. Because the company was so small, Max quickly found himself a senior employee with lots of responsibilities. As the company grew and expanded its reach into other countries, Max found himself in a senior position heading up international marketing sales and operations. He traveled around the world, setting up sales offices in Europe, Japan, Korea, and Australia. "I was king of the world," Max recounts.

At the same time that his career at Google was taking off, Max became interested in meditation. When he meditated he felt calm and more grounded, and found that life seemed to work better. But as he continued meditating, he started becoming more aware and explicit about what was important to him in life. Instead of merely trying to improve himself so he could be better at his job at Google, Max found that he wanted something else. "All the things that were supposed to be making me happy, like money, recognition, sex, and expensive meals, weren't really doing the job," Max reflects. In meditation, Max was finding a way to get in touch with something more essential about his life and what was truly important to him.

Max practiced meditation in the mornings before work and regularly attended weekend meditation retreats. Even though he was traveling a lot he still kept up with his practice, following the credo, "If you have time to breathe, you have time to meditate." As Max got more and more into meditation, he eventually decided that he wanted to dedicate himself more fully to Buddhism.

Then came the big moment. In order to really honor what mattered to him, Max would need to leave Google and train to become a Buddhist priest. While most people were supportive of his decision, albeit a little surprised, one senior manager at Google told him, "You'll be back." According to Max, this senior manager had two main passions in life: to make a lot of money and to be involved in new technology. So working at Google was right for him. But these were not Max's most important values, and he knew that he had to follow his own. "One of the biggest lessons I learned was that you have to fully align your actions with your values. It's the only way to be on the right path."

Did Max make the right decision to walk away from untold riches and power at Google to pursue a life that might be considered quite mundane by comparison? Values are an extremely personal thing. What's important and meaningful for one person may not be for another. It's only when we are clear about and living true to our own values that we will be happy, fulfilled, and truly successful.

We are always operating under a set of values that guide our behaviors in any given situation. When I hold the door open for someone who just held it open for me, the value of reciprocity is likely in effect. But as with purpose, most people are not aware of the values that are driving their behaviors in most situations. Instead, their behaviors are being determined by default values that may or may not be optimal for the situation at hand. *Operating from a clear set of values, which are specially chosen for a given context, will improve your ability to execute and increase your likelihood of success.*

DEFINING YOUR VALUES

Our values are the underlying principles that dictate our behavior. I like to phrase these principles as behaviors to make the link to action crystal clear. And in the way I am using them they can and should change depending on the context. For example, my values for being a parent are different from my core values for being a CEO or a politician, because the behaviors that will guide us to success in each of these areas are different.

Core Values

While we all have many principles that are important to us, not all values are created equal. Some are more central than others; these are known as "core values." They are the beliefs that most orient you above all else. We usually stick to four core values, which together with a purpose statement create a kind of code of being for us. Any more than this, and we can start to lose track of what our core values actually are.

Values Alignment

Lack of fulfillment is often caused by a misalignment in values. If you are not honoring the principles that are most important to you, life will not feel so good. You will have that persistent feeling that you are missing out on something, that others have what you don't, and you will feel energetically drained, because you're not actually doing what gives you energy. Making sure our actions are aligned with our values is essential to feeling fulfilled, to operating at maximum energy, and to setting our-selves up for success.

Conflicting Values

Sometimes even when our values are aligned, when we're living accord-ing to the principles that matter most, we can still feel stuck. Usually this is because two or more of our values are in conflict with each other. If I am a leader of a team, I may feel stuck around a decision to bring some-one in from the outside versus promoting someone from within. This stuckness stems from the conflict of my value of "achieving results" with "building trust." I can move past this impasse by recognizing the values that are in tension, seeing if I can find a way to honor them both, and if not, getting clear on which value is of higher priority. Per-haps involving the team in the process of bringing in someone external would be a way of honoring both values and moving forward.

System Values

My work as a therapist and business coach revolves around helping people and organizations achieve their potential. Much of this focuses on how to optimize oneself or one's organization to achieve results. However, the environment in which people and organizations exist matters. If the underlying values of the environment you are in are counter to your values for success, you will be like Sisyphus perpet-ually pushing a boulder uphill. So whether it's your job or where you live make sure the values of the external environment support you in achieving your goals.

Values don't just guide us to what we might need to walk away from, as in the case of Max Erdstein and Google. They also provide powerful guidance for how we should be spending our time. Here's an example of how values give us the motivation and energy to go full tilt when we need to.

CHARLIE CHEN, FOUNDER, MACRO-VEGETARIAN FOODS

When your values tell you to put in twenty hours a day

Charlie Chen became a vegetarian and couldn't find anything he liked to eat outside of what he prepared at home. So he decided to start a company that would make and distribute healthy vegetarian food. At the time of our conversation, he had more than forty-five products that could be found in supermarkets and health food stores all over New York City, including giants like Fairway, Whole Foods, Gourmet Garage, and others. His vision was to take the company national within the year.

Even though his business was so successful that he could retire if he wanted, Charlie was still driving one of the company delivery trucks seven days a week. On an average day, Charlie is at his office at 7 a.m., hits the road for deliveries by 9 a.m., and doesn't get home until late into the evening. When I asked him why he still drives a truck and works so hard, he said it was because he loves what he does.

Before starting Macro-Vegetarian Foods, Charlie was in the restaurant business and was doing quite well financially. But he began to ask himself, "So what?" "I wasn't doing anything I believed in, and I was tired. A job makes you tired because you have to do it, not because you want to do it. My business now is exactly in line with my values, so it is so easy for me to stay excited about it. I just want to keep making our food better tasting and more nutritious for people."

I met Charlie about midway through his schedule of deliveries. It had rained all morning and was particularly gray and rainy, one of those days you just want to stay in bed. However,

Charlie seemed totally unaffected. He was laughing and full of energy.

When I asked Charlie if there were ever times that he got discouraged, he told me how hard things were during the first two years of business. "When we first started, there weren't too many health food stores, and the health consciousness we see today hadn't really started yet. Stores that I tried to sell to said they weren't interested. The gourmet stores didn't want to be bothered." But with persistence, and growing demand for healthy vegetarian alternatives, Macro-Foods was picked up by a few health food stores and was able to just barely scrape by. "I did everything those first couple of years," Charlie recalls with a smile. "I cooked. I cleaned. I drove the truck. But this is what I believe in, so I did not give up."

When I ask Charlie what advice he would give to someone who would like to bring more fulfillment to their lives, he answers simply: "Always ask yourself, is this something I really love? If the answer is yes, do it with everything you have. If you are really passionate about something, working twenty hours a day is not that much. If you really love it, show that you love it by doing it to the maximum!" While spending time in ways that aren't aligned with your values makes you tired and leaves you unfulfilled, aligning your values and time will leave you bursting with energy and joy for what you're doing.

Now that we're clear on what values are, the principles that guide our behaviors, you're ready to begin coming up with your own sets of values, to assess whether you're living in alignment with them, and to narrow the gaps and resolve any conflicts between them. Below are exercises that will guide you through this process.

YOUR TURN—VALUES EXERCISES

Values Inventory

Step 1. Make a list of ten to twenty activities that are most important to you. These could be things such as "spending time with friends and family," "exercising," "being outdoors," etc.

Step 2. Assign a rating from 1–10 (10 being the highest) of how *important* each activity is to you currently.

Step 3. Next, rate each from 1–10 according to how much you are currently doing/living that thing.

Step 4. For each activity that you listed, subtract the doing/living score from the importance score.

Step 5. Take a look. What are the things you value most? Where are the biggest gaps?

Step 6. Go through the list and write down steps you could take to bring the two scores into closer alignment (i.e., when the two scores equal each other).

Step 7. Make some commitments and start living a more values-aligned life.

CHAPTER FOUR

Vision—
The Third Peak
Performance Pillar

"If you don't know where you're going, any road will get you there."
—LEWIS CARROLL

I f values are the oars that do the work of rowing us to our destination, then vision is the destination. Let's delve into the third pillar of our Peak Performance Formula.

Vision is a clear and compelling picture of what you want. It helps ensure you are expending your time and energy en route to the right destination. It also helps you set the right context for the shorter-term goals you set for yourself. As the quote above captures, having a clear vision prevents us from meandering through life, wandering down whatever road presents itself. This chapter shares the power and process of creating a vision and the goal-setting that follows.

NANCY MEYERS COOLIDGE, COFOUNDER, BEACON HILL VILLAGE

Reenvisioning the future of aging in America

Beacon Hill Village (beaconhillvillage.org) is a nonprofit organization located in Boston that helps seniors stay in their homes as they age, which according to surveys is what most seniors want. "I don't want a so-called expert determining how I should be treated or what should be available to me," one of Beacon Hill's founders explains. "The thing I most cherish here is that it's we, the older people, who are creating our own universe."

At the time of my conversation with Nancy, Beacon Hill Village had approximately 340 members of ages ranging from fifty-two to ninety-eight years. Members pay annual dues, with funds raised from local foundations and from wealthier members subsidizing the dues for moderate and low-income members. Dues cover basic needs like weekly trips to the supermarket, rides from volunteers, and home delivery of meals from local restaurants. At additional cost, usually at a discount, members have access to services such as home repairs, home health aides, and personal trainers.

In addition to providing for these more basic needs, Beacon Hill Village also coordinates activities to keep members engaged, challenged, and connected to the outside world. For physical activity, Beacon Hill offers group exercise classes and tai chi. For intellectual stimulation and social interaction, members can go to lectures and social gatherings, attend brain and memory programs, and have volunteering opportunities. They also are offered outings to the Botanical Gardens, Boston Pops, Boston Opera, and Boston Ballet as well as trips to the Berkshires, Tanglewood, and Martha's Vineyard.

Beacon Hill Village was founded by a dozen local residents who wanted to find a way to stay at home as they aged. They did not want to be dependent on their adult children or move to a retirement community or assisted living center. Retirement, illness, and losing a spouse or close friend are all major challenges for seniors. Add to those the pressure that adult children often place on older parents to move into assisted living centers or nursing homes before they truly need to, and it's easy for seniors to start to doubt their own ability to take care of themselves.

Nancy Meyers Coolidge is one of Beacon Hill's founders and is a social worker by training. She understands the dynamics of aging. "You have to be out in the world, using your body and brain, and doing something meaningful, otherwise you will not be happy," Nancy said when I asked her what she thought were the keys for staying motivated as seniors face the challenges of aging. "No one wants to be told they're old and can't do things. There's lots of depression associated with aging as one loses their abilities, friends, and family. So you need activities that you care about and that are intellectually and physically challenging. Not just knitting or bingo, but activities that connect you to what's going on in the world."

According to a *New York Times* article about Beacon Hill Village, "Community-based models for aging in place designed by the people who use them are the wave of the future." Nancy envisioned a different reality she wanted for herself and others who were aging. Vision was the first critical step to bringing what did not yet exist into being.

DEFINING VISION

Vision is the ability to create clarity around something you would like to happen in the future that hasn't happened yet. The more clear and detailed the vision the easier it is to make it happen. Here's a pretty clear example of how an Olympic athlete used a simple-but-powerful form of visioning to help her reach her goal. When she was five years old, the swimmer Missy Franklin drew a picture of herself on the podium, receiving a gold medal at the Olympics. It began as a picture in her childhood room, but twelve years later she won four gold medals at the 2012 Olympic Games.

> **Visioning is not predicting the future.**
> **Rather it is getting clear about what you want life to be**
> **like or what you want to accomplish in a given area.**

Setting a vision creates clarity between where you would like to be and where you are now. Once a vision has been established, it can be as if the mind starts moving you in that direction almost unconsciously. Aspects of your vision can start coming to fruition seemingly without effort. These instances can feel a bit uncanny. I don't recommend leaving things up to your unconscious mind here. And this is where setting goals and consistently monitoring progress helps to more intentionally make your vision a reality. I'll show you how to do this later in this chapter. But first let's look at how visioning works.

How Visioning Works

To better understand how visioning works, let's examine a type of visioning practice known as visualization, which has been used for purposes such as enhancing athletic performance as well as fighting disease. Visualization is the process of imagining yourself performing in your ideal state. Neurologically, this process builds and strengthens neural networks that are the road map for successful performance. We know from imaging studies of the brain that imagining an action activates the same areas of the brain as actually doing the actions. So you essentially create a film in you mind of you performing flawlessly, and then rehearse this performance over and over.

One study of world-class athletes demonstrates the power of visualization. Athletes were divided into four groups with the following breakdown of their training program:

1. 100 percent physical training
2. 75 percent physical training and 25 percent visualization
3. 50 percent physical training and 50 percent visualization
4. 25 percent physical training and 75 percent visualization.

The last group showed the greatest improvement in performance, even though they did substantially less physical training than any other group.

When the *Survivor: Africa* winner Ethan Zohn was a professional soccer player, he used visualization to help him focus and get game-ready. He would visualize himself in specific high-pressure, high-stress moments of a game and see himself performing successfully in those situations. Later, when he was battling cancer, he continued to use visualization as a tool to activate his body's immune system and maintain a positive outlook. He says, "I believed if I put good, happy, purposeful goal-setting thoughts and visions in my head before going to bed, my mind and body would work for me when I slept." Visualization can be used for maintaining confidence, refining technique, or preparing for contingencies.

As with visualization, visioning can be done for very short time horizons or specific goals like improving athletic performance in a competition. Or it can be used for longer-term life planning. In my coaching practice clients often find it immensely helpful to get more clear on their vision twenty years into the future and to make sure that what they are doing now is moving them in that direction. For a guided visioning process to meet yourself twenty years from now go to the end of the chapter.

Goal-Setting

Once we've created a longer-term vision for ourselves, we can start setting goals that help us achieve that vision. Setting the right goals allows us to create a plan and design accountability around progress and results.

An often-cited Harvard University study found that people who committed their goals to writing were more likely to achieve them than those who merely held them as aspirations. There is something so powerful about thoughtfully setting and committing to goals. Here's how I do it.

SMART Goals

Setting the right goals is monumentally important. I am reminded of the question "What good is it if you solve the wrong problem?" Good goal-setting takes practice. It requires us to do some deep thinking about what is most important to us, what is aspirational and also realistic. Many of us have heard of SMART goals as a good set of guidelines for goal-setting. The SMART goal system was first developed by GE in the 1940s. It held that goals must be Specific, Measurable, Achievable, Realistic, and Timebound. And in fact, studies show that setting goals in this way leads to a higher performance than abstract goals.

The process I have found most useful for goal-setting, implementing, and monitoring progress is adapted from a practice called Objectives and Key Results (OKRs). OKRs were developed at Intel and Google, and are used by many organizations. I like OKRs for their simplicity and cohesion. Here's how my process works.

1. Set your annual goals.

Look at your vision, and based on where you currently are ask yourself, "At the end of this year, what do I want to have accomplished?" Three goals is probably enough and five should be the upper limit. These should be not only aspirational but also attainable, and reflect the most important areas of your life for the upcoming year.

2. Set your Objectives and Key Results monthly.

From your annual goals create three to five monthly Objectives. These are basically goals for the month that will move you toward attaining your annual goals. Next, for each Objective select three to five Key Results that, if achieved that month, will add up to the achievement of that Objective. Key Results should be quantifiable, so you can assess to what extent you did them.

3. Monitor and score your OKRs weekly.

Each week review your OKRs. Put "Review OKRs" in your calendar on weekly repeat, so you remember to do it. Give yourself a score for each Key Result on a scale of 0 to 1 (0 means you didn't do it all; 1 means you totally achieved it.) This gives you a sense of where you need to focus more attention next week.

4. Score and reflect on your OKRs at the end of each month.

At the end of the month, average the Key Results. That is your Objective Score. Reflect on where you were successful and where you weren't. Your score will tell you if you need to continue with an Objective for the next month or if it's time to set a new one.

Do a six-month revision of your annual goals based on any changes that have occurred in the prior half of the year. Reflect on how the year went and what it means for the next year. Repeat this process annually. By creating a clear and compelling vision, then breaking that vision down into more bite-size goals, monitoring progress, and making needed adjustments along the way, we can increase our chances of manifesting the life we dream of.

Now that I've taken you through the basic foundational material, we can begin exploring how these elements come into play in real-life situations with the Peak Performance Formula. But first, here are activities to start building your visualization, visioning, and goal-setting skills.

YOUR TURN—VISUALIZATION AND VISIONING EXERCISES

Visualization

Visualization works best when the images you evoke include movement rather than static images.

1. Begin by establishing a specific goal of something you would like to improve performance in. It could be a work meeting or presentation, a difficult conversation with your partner, or your serve, jump shot, or other athletic activity.

2. Find a quiet place where you will be uninterrupted, sit or lie down, and begin breathing slowly and deeply from your belly.

3. Begin to imagine the scene, using all of your senses to make it as vivid as possible. Where are you? What is around you? What does the air feel like, what smells are in the air? What sounds do you hear?

4. Now imagine yourself doing the activity flawlessly, increment by increment, like you are watching a slow-motion replay of a video. If you do make a mistake, stop the video, rewind, and go back and do it again the way you would like to do it.

5. Notice what emotions you are feeling, and what sensations you are feeling in your body.

6. Continue breathing slowly and deeply.

7. After running through the activity three or four times, you should be able to run through it effortlessly. When you can do this, choose a cue word that will elicit this visualization for you.

Strive to practice your visualization three (or more) times each week for ten to fifteen minutes.

Three- to Six-Month Vision

This activity is good for relatively short-term goal-setting.

Think about where you want to be in three to six months and really imagine yourself there. This time frame is far enough out to be meaningful, but not too far to be vague and out of reach. Write down what you see. Next, from this list pick the highest leverage things you want to achieve. By high leverage, I mean that accomplishing the thing will make the biggest difference in your life and/or will help you realize the greatest number of things that matter most to you. Since you won't be able to accomplish everything on your list, choose one or two of the highest leverage goals to work on. For example, getting physically fit tends to be a high leverage goal, since it provides us with more energy and confidence for all the other parts of our life. Perhaps you see yourself running a half marathon this summer after a relatively inactive winter.

Future-Self Visioning: Guided Visualizations

We can use guided visualizations to help us gain clarity on where we are going in life and what we want for ourselves in the longer term, as well as to get clear on the steps that will set us on a path to get there.

The Time Machine

1. Sit back, relax, and get comfortable. Close your eyes and take some deep breaths, in and out—full inhalations followed by complete exhalations, pushing those last bits of air out of your abdomen.

2. Feel your weight in the chair that's supporting your body, providing welcome relief to the pressures of your day. Scan your body to see if you are holding any tension, and then consciously let go of that tension. Check your jaw, neck, shoulders, legs, and feet. Just relax.

   You are about to go on a journey. You are excited, but you are also calm and relaxed. The chair you're in is no ordinary chair. It is a time machine that will be taking you into the future, to see your life then and to meet your future self, the best version of you, many years from now. As you prepare for this journey, you remember another journey you've taken, a walk or a hike that led you to stand before a lake or a pond. You remember picking up a rock and throwing it into the water, watching the ripples of water spread out in concentric circles. The water is so clear, you can see the stone sinking to the bottom, going down, and finally resting on the soft sandy ground, just sitting there, not doing anything. Just like you are sitting comfortably in the chair of this time machine. You will effortlessly take the controls and guide yourself on this journey.

3. Take another full breath, in and out. Placing your hand on the control, begin to feel the quantum effects of the time machine taking hold. Your consciousness contains all of time and reality, past, present, and future. Finally, you touch down in the future in the place where you live, many years from now.

4. Take a moment to situate yourself, knowing that in just another moment you will be stepping out into the world where your best you resides. Step outside and look around. Notice what you see, the type of environment you are in. Notice what is striking or stands out to you. You are within short walking distance of your future self's home. Take it in and notice what it looks like. Make your way to the entrance and knock on the door. When it opens,

your future self, who has figured it all out, will be there. What do you look like? What kind of energy do you have? Your future self invites you in and ushers you to the most comfortable part of the house, the best place for a conversation. You're offered a drink, and while you are waiting you look around. You look at the photos on the wall, and you see the people and experiences that have been most meaningful to you over the years. Who and what do you see?

5. Your future self returns, and you sit down together to talk. Your future self really has things figured out and under control. And that makes you feel safe and relaxed. Safe and relaxed enough to ask these two questions: What do I need to do to get where you are? (Take a moment to wait for the answer. Good.) What do I need to change or let go of? (Because you know it is safe, you can really be open to the answer. Good.)

6. You have time to ask your future self one more question. What is something you're unsure about that you'd like an answer to? Go ahead and ask.

7. It's time to say goodbye. Before you go, your future self gives you something—something to remind you of the one who has things figured out and everything under control. It could be a keepsake or a special nickname that helps you easily connect with this state of being. Accept this gift before you go.

8. Say goodbye in whatever way feels right and make your way back to the time machine. Settle in and prepare to return to the present. Make sure you have everything you want to take back with you from this journey. Check the controls to make sure all systems are go. Pull back on the throttle and feel the slow movement of time travel begin. Sit back and relax while you are carried back to present day. Know that when you open your eyes, you will feel rested and refreshed, like you've had a good nap.

9. Open your eyes, look around, stretch your body, and spend a few minutes collecting your thoughts or taking notes on these questions:

What did your future surroundings and house look like?

What did your future self have figured out and under control?

Who and what did you see in the pictures?

What did you most need to keep in mind to get from where you are now to where your future self resides?

What do you need to change or let go of?

What question did you ask and what was the answer?

What was the keepsake or name that captures the essence of who you are when you've got it all figured out and everything is under control?

Based on the experience you had in the time machine exercise, I invite you to create a more detailed vision for yourself. Describe in more detail (at least a short paragraph for each) what your life will look like twenty years from now in each of the categories below:

Health

Family

Career/Impact

Money

Geography (where you live, the home you live in, etc.)

Passions and hobbies

Goal-Setting: Personal Objectives and Key Results (OKRs)

Based on the above visioning exercises, identify three to five annual goals that you most want to accomplish by the end of this year. (Example: End this year the healthiest I've ever been.)

1. _____

2. _____

3. _____

4. _____

5. _____

Based on these goals, identify three to five Objectives you want to be your main focus for the next one-to-three-month period. For each Objective, provide three to five Key Results that together will result in your achieving your Objective. Review your Key Results weekly to ensure you are making adequate progress to achieve your Objective within the time period you've committed to.

Congratulations, you're on your way to creating the life you've always dreamed of!

PART II

Applying the Formula to
Achieve Your Potential

CHAPTER FIVE

Becoming a Peak Performer

JIM COURIER, FORMER WORLD NUMBER ONE-TENNIS PLAYER

Doing the work

One of the best ways to improve our performance is to learn from those who have cracked the code of peak performance and realized their highest potential. Jim Courier has without question done this. As a professional tennis player he spent fifty-eight weeks as the number-one ranked tennis player in the world, four years ranked in the world top ten, and won twenty-six singles and six doubles titles, including back-to-back championships at the Australian Open and back-to-back championships at the French Open. Over the thirteen years of his professional tennis career, Courier was known for his punishing ground strokes and his drive to win.

When Jim was a kid, he would hit tennis balls against a wall for hours on end. "The wall was the ultimate test. It never missed." He never tired of hitting balls against the wall and would continue for as long as his parents would let him. When the sun went down and his mom and dad came to get him, he was not happy and would go home reluctantly. "Early on, my goal was to become the best tennis player I could be." As he got older, he became more aware of competition and winning.

But as important as winning was to Courier, it never eclipsed his desire to perfect his game. "We all have a public scorecard with which we measure ourselves, which is the win or the loss. But you can play your best tennis and still lose. So for sanity purposes, most great players also set personal goals for themselves, like improving footwork or working on a specific shot, like your overhead." When I expressed surprise that the best tennis players in the world still focused on the basics like overheads, he replied, "You have to get microscopic to perfect something."

When I asked Courier if he'd ever lost his drive for tennis, he told me that his love of tennis, like most things in life, ebbs and flows. "We all go through times when we're tired, overplayed, and over-traveled and are handed some tough loses. In a particular match, you might be disappointed by calls or with the way you're playing. But it's the player who has trained their mind to deal with those situations by getting less carried away by the highs and lows who can tough it out."

This interview with Courier highlights the key aspects of what it takes to achieve peak performance, achieving mastery in three areas: the physical, the technical, and the mental. But first we need to make sure we are able to access the full range of resources available to us.

BRING YOUR WHOLE SELF TO THE TASK

We all have parts of ourselves that have not been fully developed, that have been neglected, or that we've been compelled to disown as "not us." In some cases we were not exposed to certain ways of being much or at all. In other cases we shed parts of ourselves to gain acceptance, a sense of belonging, and to get to where we've gotten in life thus far. And in more extreme cases we've disowned or denied parts of ourselves because it was not emotionally (and sometimes physically) safe to express those parts. And similar to plants, what doesn't have fertile soil, water, and light in our emotional life fails to grow.

Why does this matter? you might ask. *I'm getting along fine.* But you are missing out on your full range of being, not being true to who you really are, and are not using all the resources you have at your disposal to achieve your goals. Like being an athlete with only one type of game, you are limiting your range and are not living up to your potential. For many of us, the very aspects of ourselves that are less accessible directly impede our ability to perform at our highest levels and to feel full fulfillment while doing it.

How do we reclaim what we've done such a good job of disavowing, that we are so out of touch with, that we don't even know what it is? The exercises that come later will help you identify, get back in touch with, and start to reactivate key parts of yourself, allowing you to reclaim your whole self. With our whole selves at our command, and the heightened self-awareness of who we truly are, we can more effectively do the work it takes to get better and enjoy it more. The core components of this work are outlined next.

Mastering the Three Key Components of Peak Performance

There is no substitute for putting in the time and effort to reach elite levels. Peak performance by definition means you are an expert. That in some area you know more or can do more than most everyone else. Experts, by definition, have developed specific methods for thinking and acting. One of the earliest studies of expertise compared chess masters to very good chess players. Both groups were shown examples of chess games and asked to think aloud as they decided what moves they would make. Both groups showed considerable breadth and depth in their thinking. What set the chess masters apart was that they considered higher quality moves than those contemplated by the less-experienced players.

The researchers found that experts have a different way of viewing the world that allows them to consistently outperform their opponents. They are better able to recognize meaningful patterns and their implications. Experts tend to organize their knowledge around "big ideas." These big ideas allow them to stay engaged with incredibly complex challenges in ways that novices cannot.

In another study, physics experts and college students were asked to describe how they would go about solving various physics problems. College students typically described the equations they would use and how they would manipulate them. The experts typically began with the major principles or laws that applied to the problem, along with a rationale for why and how they could be applied. If a college student chose the wrong equation, they were much more likely to get lost and frustrated—they did not have the expert's road map to follow.

Experts are also superior at retrieving the knowledge they need when they need it. Retrieval ability varies from effortful to relatively effortless (fluent) to automatic. Fluent and automatic retrieval are characteristics of expertise. Learning to speak a foreign language provides a useful example. Beginners must literally translate every word in their heads before they speak. With enough practice, speaking takes place without thinking and becomes automatic. Experts have gotten so good at whatever they do that it has become relatively effortless. This is why masters make difficult things look so easy.

Regardless of what is being mastered, it takes a significant amount of time to gain mastery. It is estimated that ten thousand hours of practice is required to achieve mastery associated with being a world-class expert in anything. That's roughly three hours a day, twenty hours a week, over ten years. No one has yet found a case in which true world-class expertise was accomplished in less time. It has been estimated that world-class chess players require from fifty thousand to one hundred thousand hours of practice to reach that level of expertise; they rely on a knowledge base containing fifty thousand chess patterns to guide their selection of moves. Much of this time involves developing fluent identification of meaningful patterns of information. Time and practice are the keys to becoming a peak performer in three very specific areas: the physical, the technical, and the mental.

The Physical: Manage Energy and Recover Like a Peak Performer

Without the levels of energy and stamina to put in the hard work, you will not be able to excel, in sports, business, or anywhere. This is where sleep, diet, exercise, and training come into play.

A trend I have been following over the years is the increased focus on energy management and recovery in athletics. This focus has allowed athletes to compete harder for longer, pushing back typical retirement ages five to ten years depending on the sport. Serena Williams at thirty-nine years old had played professional tennis for twenty-six years. LeBron James was in his seventeenth NBA season at age thirty-five, Roger Federer had been playing professional tennis for twenty-two years at age thirty-eight, and Tom Brady had played twenty seasons in the NFL at age forty-two. One thing they have in common that has allowed them this kind of sustained excellence (besides amazing genetics) is their enhanced focus on managing their energy and recovery. This focus has begun to make its way to other areas of performance. Let's delve into a few areas I have found to be most universally beneficial.

PRIORITIZE SLEEP

Aim for at least seven to nine hours of sleep each night. Ten hours is not too much, especially when your body or mind have been under extreme stress. When we sleep our brains replay, process, learn, and extract meaning. Getting adequate sleep enhances performance. In a 2011 study, basketball players at Stanford University were asked to sleep as much as possible for seven weeks. On average, they slept an additional two hours, compared to their usual sleep routine. The researchers observed that the players sprinted 4 percent faster, shot free throws and three pointers with 9 percent better accuracy, and demonstrated faster reaction time. For a business example, Jeff Bezos, the founder of Amazon, prioritizes getting eight hours of sleep each night, because sleep improves the quality of his interactions and decisions.

NAPPING

Although it's not yet acceptable in our grind-it-out work culture, napping is one of the best restorative practices you can engage in. I used to think napping was a lazy person's luxury, but when I had kids and lots of nights of interrupted sleep, I began napping out of necessity. Then I started reading the research and soon became a convert. A NASA study found that pilots who napped for up to forty-five minutes showed a 34 percent improvement in reaction time and a twofold improvement in alertness. Further, napping has been shown to boost short-term memory as well as associative memory (the type of memory that allows us to match a face with a name). Napping also helps to strengthen the immune system and even anticipating a nap can reduce blood pressure. Most people start to get tired sometime in the afternoon. A nap at this time can help to restore you and refuel you for the rest of the day. The research says that ten-to- thirty-minute naps yield the greatest benefits without the grogginess of deeper sleep.

TAKE BREAKS

We can only maintain focused attention for about ninety minutes to two hours at a time. After this our focus is not optimal, and we begin to feel fatigued, slow down, lose creativity, and make mistakes. In one study, those who took as little as a six-minute walk outdoors increased their creativity by more than 60 percent versus those who remained seated at their desks.

We should strategically insert longer break periods to follow higher periods of stress. Vacations lasting seven to ten days have positive effects on motivation, well-being, and health that last up to one month.

ALIGN TASKS WITH TIME OF DAY

Our cognitive abilities do not remain static over the course of a day. And these daily fluctuations are more extreme than we realize with the low point being equivalent to the effect of drinking the legal limit of alcohol. Time of day effects can explain 20 percent of the variance in human performance on cognitive undertakings. Mental keenness as shown by evaluating evidence is greater early in the day. Our "inhibitory control" is better earlier in the day, and this helps our brains solve analytical problems by keeping out distractions. For most of us, sharp-minded analytic capacities peak in the late morning or around noon. Later in the day, we excel at tasks where creative insight is needed that requires less inhibition and resolve.

SINGLE TASK

The brain can focus on only one thing at a time. The process of multitasking actually involves switching between tasks or allotting only a portion of our cognitive capacity to a specific task. Switching costs add up and can eat up as much as 40 percent of our productive time and energy. Research shows that chronic multitaskers are worse at filtering out irrelevant information, slower at identifying patterns, and have worse long-term memory. So focus on only one thing at a time to be more productive and save energy.

AUTOMATE DECISIONS

Every time we make a decision, however inconsequential it may seem, our brain is processing different scenarios and evaluating options, using up energy. The average adult brain in resting state already consumes about 20 percent of the body's total energy. Identify and strive to cut out all the superficial things in your life. Say no to things, so that when it's time to say yes you can do so with all your energy. Automate as many of the decisions that don't really matter to you as you can (e.g., what to wear, what to eat, when to complete daily activities, whether to attend social activities, etc.). As the decisions add up, so, too, does the amount of energy required.

The Technical: Master Technique Like a Peak Performer

You have to be able to execute in the areas where success is determined. Whether that is Jim Courier working on his overhead, Steph Curry shooting free throws for basketball, a start-up founder raising money for his or her company, or a political candidate speaking in public—the technical skills must be mastered. Since it's much easier to master the things you're already good at, try to boost your strengths rather than focus on improving things you are not great at. In his book *Talent Is Overrated,* author Geoff Colvin studies how elite performers actually improve their skills. Here's what he learned.

DELIBERATE PRACTICE

Performance improvement is not just about practice, but deliberate practice. Deliberate practice is an activity specifically designed to improve performance—reaching for objectives just beyond our current ability, providing feedback on results, and involving high levels of repetition. Deliberate practice is what separates ordinary from world-class performers. "The best performers," says Colvin, "set goals that are not about the outcome, but about the process of reaching the outcome." Let's look at the components of deliberate practice more closely.

Deliberate design: The first key to deliberate practice is to specifically design an activity to improve your performance. This involves focusing on a specific aspect of what you are trying to learn and keeping at it until there is improvement before moving on to the next skill. Colvin points out that it is almost always necessary for a teacher or coach to design the activity that is best suited to improve our performance, especially in the early stages of development. While we may eventually become skilled enough to design our own practice, good teachers will know the latest and best methods for us given our current skill level.

Stretching it: The second key to deliberate practice involves stretching ourselves beyond our current ability. This usually means practicing something we are not very good at. Colvin points out that this isn't much fun, and therefore most people don't practice this way. Instead, they do what they are already able to do, which is why they don't improve much.

Feedback: The third component of deliberate practice is that the results of our practice are continuously available to us for evaluation. World-class chess players practice by replaying games played by former champions, choosing a move and then looking at what the champion did. In this way, feedback allows us to evaluate what we are doing and make necessary adjustments to improve.

Repetition: Finally, there is no substitute for doing lots of an activity we are trying to learn. Repetition, when done with focus and concentration, helps us consolidate and refine new skills. However, if the activity does not isolate a specific aspect of what we are trying to learn, if it does not stretch us, and if we aren't receiving feedback from which to make adjustments, we can practice as much as we want, and we probably won't improve much.

Across disciplines, four or five hours a day seems to be the upper limit of deliberate practice, usually in practice sessions of no more than an hour to ninety minutes at a time. Commit to this process and see your technique improve dramatically.

The Mental: Adopt a Peak Performance Mindset

At the elite level, what sets people apart? Everyone can have the training and skill to be the best, but the difference maker is all in the mind—the ability to control it, keep it focused, and keep it positive. You don't need to be an elite performer to benefit. With a peak performance mindset it is amazing what you can achieve.

MARTIN STREL, LONG-DISTANCE SWIMMER

The power of the mind

On April 7, 2007, Martin Strel completed a 3,274-mile swim of the Amazon River, setting a new world record. Over sixty-six days, Martin battled elements including whirlpools, piranhas, alligators, snakes, spiders, oncoming boats, and pirates. Why did he do this? Is he crazy?

Martin had long been interested in water, swimming, and rivers. He started swimming when he was five years old. When he was old enough, Martin began competing as a professional long-distance swimmer. "Instead of racing with the same people in the same places, I wanted to do something different." So Martin swam his first river, the Krka, a sixty-five-mile river in his home country of Slovenia. "When I was a kid, the water in the river was very clean. But when I was swimming, I noticed how polluted it had become. I decided to dedicate my river swims to peace, friend- ship, and clean water." Next Martin swam the Mississippi, Yangtze, and Danube rivers. But the mighty Amazon was the Mount Everest of rivers, and he wanted to be the first person to swim it.

Martin prepared for more than two years for the Amazon swim. In addition to training, Martin assembled a team around him to help plan logistics, doctors to care for his health, security to keep him safe from pirates, and others to support him through the ups and downs of the swim. Every day the team got together to discuss the progress, obstacles, and plans for the next day, which helped keep Martin relaxed and focused.

When we spoke about what above all else helped Martin achieve his goal, he talked about focus and concentration. "Your mind is the strongest muscle in your body." In order to swim for twelve hours a day, Martin would enter a state of deep concentration that allowed him to handle the pain that he was feeling in his body. "It's almost like taking a nap while I'm swimming," describes Martin. "When I 'wake up' I feel reborn, fresh, and without any pain." This ability has taken Martin many years to develop. He advises trying to build concentration little by little, practicing getting into a state of deep concentration and staying in this state longer each time you try.

According to Martin, many people make the mistake of giving up their dream too soon. They don't have the self-confidence to keep going. "Never think, 'I can't do this.'" This will become a self-fulfilling prophecy.

Even with his positive attitude and some of the world's longest rivers under his belt, there were times when Martin did not know if he could finish. A few times they had to throw buckets of blood overboard to distract piranhas, and Martin got sick from swallowing water and came down with a case of dengue fever. "I was asking myself if I chose too big a challenge and if I might actually lose my life over this. But immediately I received the answer: NO!" Along the way, Martin continually reminded himself that this was the mighty Amazon River and it could not be easy to overcome. If it were, someone else would have already done it.

"I did it right," Martin says. "The only way you grow as a person is to aim for bigger challenges in your life." Martin believes that everyone has at least one thing they care deeply about (i.e., your purpose). And following this thing as far as it will take you always brings achievement and satisfaction. By honing your mind's ability to focus, endure, and stay positive, like Martin, you can achieve amazing things. (To learn more about Martin's incredible story, check out his website, amazonswim.com, or his book, *The Man Who Swam the Amazon.*)

TRAIN YOUR MIND

The mind is more important than the body as Martin points out, especially when it comes to elite performance. We need to train our minds to have a peak performance orientation. This is a mind that can focus attention, remain positive in the face of challenge, deal with stress, silence the doubt and criticism from the outside and from within, and overcome the fear of failure.

Ten years ago, I would have been sheepish to recommend meditation to people even though it's bestowed enormous benefits on me. (I have been meditating for more than twenty years, studied at monasteries in Vietnam, and have completed various three- and ten-day silent retreats.) Now, with the advent of brain imaging and advances in neuroscience, plus a growing cultural acceptance of mindfulness, so much good evidence that meditation works is out there that I recommend it more adamantly.

Meditation studies show improvements in focus, stress management and resilience, and even immune functioning. One eight-week study of a meditation program showed an improved reaction to flu shot immunity. Another study of longtime meditators showed systematic differences in brain function; gamma oscillations—associated with problem-solving and insights—were much longer than in ordinary people. Brains of people given two weeks of compassion training showed increased activation in the reward and empathy centers of the brain as well as more altruistic behavior compared to those who got two weeks of cognitive behavior therapy (which focuses on making people aware of inaccurate or negative thinking, so they can respond in more effective ways). Reports show that as little as eight minutes of meditation can produce measurable change in one's brain, while twenty minutes is thought to be the optimal session time.

Recently I spent three days at a silent retreat, practicing the Vipassana technique of meditation. This means I handed over my phone, wallet, and keys; did not eat dinner; did not talk to or look anyone in the eyes; and sat in an uncomfortable position for ten hours every day. Vipassana, which means "to see things as they really are," is the method of meditation that, as the story goes, was practiced by the Buddha himself to come out of suffering and attain enlightenment. According to this technique there are four parts of the mind:

Observing mind, which tells us something has happened that we know through our senses.

Perceiving mind, which evaluates what has happened based on our past experiences.

Sensing mind, where sensations are generated on the body out of conscious awareness. Experiences that are perceived as good get pleasant sensations, and those that are bad get unpleasant sensations.

Reacting mind, which causes us to crave the pleasant sensations (we like them and want more) and respond with aversion (we want them to stop) to unpleasant sensations. When something happens it triggers past experience. We react from those experiences and this part of our mind becomes dominant.

When we strengthen the focus of our mind through a technique known as Anapana (mindfulness of breathing) meditation, we become aware of the sensations on our bodies. The practice of Vipassana is to observe these sensations without reacting to them. By observing and not reacting, we see that all sensations, good or bad, share the same characteristic of impermanence. In other words, sooner or later they go away. At the root of what causes us to struggle is attachment from our *reacting mind* (craving for the good and aversion to the bad) to feelings that are coming and going.

So the practice is to not become attached, to not constantly react, and to let go of old stuff that keeps coming up. You are retraining your mind to not only strengthen the observing function but also to bring it into balance with the reacting function.

To be honest, the days of ten-hour Vipassana practice were one of the hardest things I've ever done. Sitting and meditating for that many hours for so many days in a row is really tough. But the results are remarkable. When I reentered the world, the same stresses and craziness were waiting for me, but they didn't have the same charge. This experience has stuck with me. Instead, those stressors roll off my shoulders and don't get to me the way they did before. I can appreciate experiences, good and bad, in a way I didn't before. But you have to keep up the training, otherwise you start reacting again and losing focus in ways that knock you off the path to your goal.

If meditation is just not for you, here are some other ways to gain more control over your mind:

Go to therapy—Release those internalized objects and recondition yourself to value your being over your doing.

Cultivate friendships and support groups—Develop and prioritize relationships that will help you reach your goals; be kind and generous to others as you would be to yourself.

Nurture your body—Move your body, exercise, don't sit all day. Eat healthy foods.

Recondition your mind—Do the Three Good Things activity (write down three good things that happen each day and how you helped make them happen). Try hypnosis.

Broaden your threshold for stress—Do practices that strengthen the relaxation response of your parasympathetic nervous system. Yoga is great for this, as is the 4-7-8 Breathing technique.

FAILURE IS FEEDBACK

As an executive coach, I work with lots of start-up leaders. Many of them are constantly living on the cusp of feeling like failures. And for good reason. These founders are trying to create something that doesn't exist. They're constantly months or even weeks away from running out of money, and they face a lot of skepticism from investors as well as pressure from competitors who may have more resources. Moreover, many founders are relatively young and mostly unproven (people of color and women founders experience even greater obstacles).

Given all this, the preoccupation with failure looms large for many entrepreneurs and in our culture in general. For many of us, this aversion is so strong that it stops us from taking the risk to pursue our idea or dream. But we have to get over this impulse in order to embrace a mindset in which we drive to continually better ourselves and achieve breakthrough performance. Today, many work cultures perpetuate an aversion to failure, even though they often state otherwise.

Companies that hold themselves as bastions of creativity and innovation have wrestled with this dilemma for decades. What it boils down to is this: how do we encourage risk taking and experimentation while still ensuring results?

Facebook's motto, "move fast and break things"; the hyper popular increase in design thinking and its basic premise of prototyping; along with the concept advocated by various companies of "failing forward," are all attempts to get people to move past the failure stigma, so they may be their best creative selves.

But these tend to be mantras that carry with them the implicit caveat "as long as you succeed," and they don't really address what people are most worried about: the stigma that failure has in our society. To fail is to be less than, to have lost it all. It is not just an action of failure, but an identification with being a failure.

We live in a goal-oriented society that values achievement over everything else. As kids, we may have been constantly told how special we were and how we were expected to do big things. We may have been praised by our parents, teachers, coaches, and peers when we performed well. But when we fell short, we weren't praised and sometimes were even ridiculed. As a result, we often measure ourselves by our achievements and not by our efforts or our passion. This emphasis on achievement leads us to avoid things we are not immediately good at, even if these pursuits can bring us real meaning and reward.

The achievement trap can be so far-reaching that a single experience of failure often makes us feel like we are failures as human beings. A setback, like missing the winning shot in the middle school basketball game, can be so stinging that we lose the confidence to take risks in other parts of our life, like trying out for a part in the school play. Although the outcomes of each situation are totally independent of each other, the pressure to achieve and the multiple ways it can deflate us are a real danger to getting better.

Closely linked to the pressure to achieve is the pressure of meeting others' expectations. Ego is where our self-worth resides. Since our ego is formed in relation to others, it is overly concerned with what others think. When our external environment places higher value on material wealth and status than on doing what we love, we will often decide to pursue money and status in order to feel successful. In this way, our ego can lead us away from our purpose. How many people want to be doctors and lawyers because they are passionate about medicine and the law, and how many choose these careers because their egos want validation? To the extent that we can understand the pressures we are under for others to think we are smart, successful, and worth some-thing and the ways in which our society measures those things, we can check our ego and make sure it is helping us pursue our purpose fully instead of what others value.

ANTIDOTES TO THE PREOCCUPATION WITH FAILURE

I encourage leaders I work with to stay focused on these three anti-dotes to the anxiety (and even the possible reality) of failure. These are grounded in the perspective that the individual is bigger than the proj-ect, initiative, or company they are working on.

1. Focus on personal growth

Are you growing personally and professionally? Are you learning about yourself and others? Are you gaining new skills that will benefit you as you continue along your journey, on your next endeavor? If you are, then don't worry so much about the short-term outcomes.

The psychologist Carol Dweck talks about the growth mindset versus the fixed mindset. The fixed mindset is all about outcomes— Did I win or lose? Did I hit my target or not? The growth mindset is more about the curiosity of engaging in interesting challenges and the fulfillment that comes from trying to figure things out.

2. Focus on impact

Impact is the effect you're having or change you're making in your community of choice. If you're making an impact, or at least trying to, it alleviates the pressure of success or failure based on metrics that are much more flimsy (and not entirely under your control) in terms of what they really say about you. Focusing on impact helps you keep in touch with the bigger picture of what you are doing (i.e., your purpose) and less susceptible to the ups and downs one experiences in any venture. Working toward anything will come with inevitable challenges, but staying focused on why you're doing what you're doing, the difference you want to make, will keep you grounded. So you have to define what impact or change you are trying to make and for what community and make sure it's sufficiently meaningful to withstand the challenges you face.

3. Cultivate meaningful relationships

No matter what is happening, you can always focus on creating deeper connections with the people around you—your colleagues, partners, investors, etc. When all is said and done, these relationships are often the most fulfilling part of everything we're spending our time doing. And the relationships you foster now will most likely come in handy down the road, assuming you are taking care to ensure they are positive.

MAKE YOURSELF FAIL-PROOF

The worry about failure in our culture is pervasive. It holds people back and causes unhealthy stress. As long as you're keeping your focus on these three simple-but-powerful principles, you can never really fail. So make yourself fail-proof by ensuring that you're growing and learning in whatever you're doing, you're having or attempting to have the impact you desire, and you're paying attention to the relationships you have the opportunity to develop along the way.

Once you have this foundation of the peak performance mindset in place let's take care of that nagging, negative, and sometimes downright nasty little critic inside yourself that can wreak havoc when it's allowed to come out and have the spotlight. Yes, I'm talking about imposter syndrome.

Transform the Imposter

Self-doubt is one of the most pervasive detractors of performance. It limits us from believing we can accomplish our goals and dreams. It often stops us from even trying, even those at the pinnacle of their craft. After writing eleven renowned books, winning three Grammy Awards, and being nominated for a Pulitzer Prize and a Tony Award, Maya Angelou said, "Each time I think 'Uh oh, they're going to find out now. I've run a game on everybody, and they're going to find me out.'" This is called "imposter syndrome." I have experienced it firsthand as a founder and CEO and in my work with high-achieving clients in my psychotherapy and coaching practices.

In 1978, two American psychologists, Pauline Clance and Suzanne Imes, coined the term "imposter syndrome" after a series of studies on high-achieving women. This term describes the feeling of phoniness many of us can feel and the belief that we are not intelligent, capable, or creative despite evidence to the contrary. We fear being found out or exposed as frauds. The anxiety we experience from these feelings often leads us to sabotage ourselves by under-cutting our confidence and even avoiding potentially rewarding challenges altogether. Many founders, especially leaders from "nontraditional" backgrounds, experience imposter syndrome every day, sometimes without even realizing exactly what is at work within them.

Where does imposter syndrome come from? Why do we so easily disregard all of our prior accomplishments and strengths that prove otherwise? How can we transform it?

WHERE IT'S COMING FROM: OUR RELATIONSHIPS WITH OTHERS.

To help explain where imposter syndrome comes from, let's switch to a different psychology principle for a moment and talk about something called "object relations theory," developed in large part by a Scottish psychoanalyst named Ronald Fairbairn. Object relations theory essentially holds that humans seek attachment, and we internalize important people in our lives as a way to establish and maintain a connection with them.

The "internal saboteur" was Fairbairn's conceptualization of how we take in the negative beliefs others have about us—which work to undercut us and what we really want—and come to believe they are our own. We do this in part not to lose connection with these important people. Being successful would, in essence, be tantamount to leaving them behind (e.g., if I become a CEO I will be leaving behind my father, who struggled in his career, etc.). Essentially, we accept these negative beliefs about ourselves to preserve our idealization of those we rely on for care and love. As Fairbairn said, "It is better to be a sinner in a world of god than to live in a world ruled by the devil."

So to connect these two theories: The origins of imposter syndrome stem from early and significant times in your life when you were made to feel inadequate or that you didn't belong. These experiences—usually with parents, grandparents, siblings, or caregivers—were communications to you that you were not enough (good enough, smart enough, pretty enough, etc.). Once these initial beliefs get established, they are reinforced over time by our parents, teachers, coaches, and groups we want to be a part of. It is the solidifying of Fairbairn's "internal saboteur."

We can even internalize family mythologies handed down from generation to generation. When I went out for my high school tennis team my freshman year, I struggled to win the last spot. Dealing with those frustrations, I remembered my grandfather's story of not making his college football team, which proved that we were not a "sports family." Instead of persevering, I quit.

Why does imposter syndrome appear, even when we know in our minds otherwise? (In other words, why would Maya Angelou say that about herself?)

Feelings of imposter syndrome get triggered when we are in new situations, are seeking acceptance, or when there is a power differential and a risk of being rejected (like applying to a school or competitive fellowship or applying for a job or going in for an interview). It can happen when people are examining us closely—say, for example, an intense interview with super writer Maya Angelou could result in her statement.

Certain types of people are especially skilled at bringing out our feelings of inadequacy. People who fall on the narcissistic spectrum—those who are grandiose on the outside but actually feel inadequate on the inside—can be especially good at provoking feelings of imposter syndrome in us. To defend against their own feelings of phoniness, they make others feel as if they don't belong.

So what can we do to overcome imposter syndrome?

1. Find the root of your imposter

   When you feel like you don't belong, can't succeed, or are a phony, ask yourself "Whose voice is this?" Think back to earlier and significant experiences when you felt inadequate or that you didn't belong. Identify other experiences that reinforced that same feeling. Name the belief you've been carrying around about yourself.

2. Rewrite the narrative

   Now that you know that these beliefs do not really belong to you and were others' insecurities and inadequacies, what beliefs do you want to hold as your own? Look at your track record of resilience, resourcefulness, and success. Use those to write a new narrative about yourself and what you're capable of.

3. Know when you are vulnerable, and actively respond to yourself

   Be aware of your imposter syndrome being triggered when you're in a new situation, especially one that is competitive on some level and you might be rejected (e.g., pitching your idea to an investor, interviewing for a new job, applying to a prestigious fellowship, etc.), and make sure to take special care of your self-confidence during these experiences. Here are some specific things you can do:

Use positive self-talk. There is strong evidence that self-talk boosts performance by increasing motivation and confidence. It helps us endure uncomfortable situations. Self-talk is most effective when it's short, specific, and consistent.

Seek out believers in you. This is always good advice, but especially so when we are putting ourselves out there and facing rejection. Make sure you are consolidating your crew of supporters and limiting inter-actions with those who don't leave you feeling so good about yourself.

Try the Three Good Things exercise. This evidence-based activity asks you to write down three good things that happen each day and how you helped make them happen. Do this for one week—you'll experience a boost in confidence for six months!

Adopt a growth mindset. The growth mindset tells us that we are always growing and that our effort is what matters most. If we are not so outcome-focused and measuring ourselves against our own progress, then we're less likely to fall victim to the imposter syndrome.

Continue working hard. There's no substitute for working hard and continuing to improve your skills and knowledge base. Competence increases confidence. So just keep at it and know you are getting better and better.

Take some comfort in knowing that many people experience similar feelings of imposterness (including people we admire and can't imagine why they would feel those feelings). Know that with some awareness and proven techniques you can, and will, transform and overcome your imposter syndrome. So get out there and conquer the world! Because you are awesome! And even though you are awesome, the world is still stressful and can sometimes be overwhelming. Up next is how to deal with all that stress.

G. LOVE, MUSICIAN

Taming the imposter

Garrett Dutton started taking acoustic guitar lessons when he was eight years old. After spending a year in college, he decided to pursue music full time, and he moved to Boston to get away from friends, family, and anything else that would distract him from his music. As a street musician, he began to hone his skill.

Between street gigs, Garrett sent demo tapes to record labels, hoping that someone would take a chance on him and his unique style, which he called hip-hop blues. "When I was young, there were only a few big record companies and MTV, so making it was a pipe dream." His idol, the bluesman John Hammond, made a career performing at coffee shops and bars, and that's all he really wanted to do. As it turned out, one of the labels Garrett sent his demo to offered him a record deal, and in 1994 he released his first album.

Garrett, better known as G. Love (along with his band Special Sauce), had been rocking audiences for the past fifteen years when we spoke. His love of performing had him playing a demanding schedule of over 150 live shows a year. A key to his successful run over the past decade and a half has been a healthy attitude about fear of failure and managing his self-doubts.

In his younger days, he would go to hip-hop parties in Philadelphia, one of the few white kids there, and rap at the open mic. Garrett explains his courageousness: "Everything is telling you don't do it. But you gotta do it. I have to prove it to myself that I love it that much. I'm sitting home writing raps all day, and now it's time to step up. You have to constantly test yourself, say, 'I got this! I'm doing it my way!' And that's how you make it real. Being a street musician gave me a lot of strength. No one can take away your gig on the street. Fear is something that everyone deals with. Stage fright or nerves before a big show are always there. Before you go on stage in front of a lot of people or with great musicians, you're asking yourself, 'Oh my god, how can I do this?' It's actually a beautiful thing. You're baring yourself, your true naked self. You get on stage, and you're totally empty. You let yourself go there, so that you can rise up and become powerful from overcoming your doubt and fear. You get energy from the crowd, and from the first note you hit, the confidence surges past the fear and doubt."

Garrett's career has not been without its challenges, and when we spoke he had recently faced perhaps the biggest of his career. Right before a major tour, Garrett was performing in freezing weather while he was already sick, and his vocal cords hemorrhaged. "I probably shouldn't have performed, but I hate canceling shows." In order to get through the tour, Garrett had to be on vocal rest, where he could not speak or practice with his band for five weeks. "I learned that you need to respect your instrument," he reflects. "And that everything can be taken away from you." After the tour ended, Garrett had surgery and, thanks to diligent rehabilitation, was ready to hit the stage again, this time being sure to pace himself for the long run.

Garrett's story is an example of someone who effectively managed his fears and self-doubts. He used his street gigs and open-mic nights to build his confidence to perform, and he consistently gave himself new challenges to grow. Instead of letting the fear of what others might think dominate, he reframed what he was doing as proving to himself that he loved it that much. Later in his career, he also learned about the value of rest and recovery, which we will get to later.

Manage Stress Like a Peak Performer

Building self-confidence is an important part of overcoming the fear and self-doubts we all have. Like G. Love being the only white kid rapping at the open mic, the challenges we undertake to build our confidence and get better will most likely push us out of our comfort zones. So we need to be able to deal with the stress that accompanies performance. To quote another rapper, Lil Wayne, "What's life without pressure?"

Stress is a part of life and a necessary part of any endeavor where we are attempting to be our best. A recent scientific discovery found that "the same nerves involved in the fight or flight response can cause permanent damage to cells responsible for producing hair color in mice." So stress really can contribute to our hair going gray faster! And it can have a host of other negative effects on us, affecting our health, mood, and ability to perform at our best. If you are racked with stress and anxiety to the point of constant overwhelm, you will never be able to reach your potential. We need to be able to transform stress, our reactions to it, and its effect on our lives to make sure it's adaptive and not destructive. Here's how:

1. Make it worth the stress.

Stress is necessary for growth and, as the quote above implies, it's unavoidable. In the rapper Lil Wayne's case, it was either going to be the stress of trying to pay the rent or something more ambitious like making hit records. As much as possible, spend your time in line with your purpose, values, and vision and know that the stress you are experiencing is helping you achieve your goals. When we view stress as a result of choices we are making, we will feel less stressed out.

2. Keep the nervous system calm.

Chronic stress leaves us feeling like we are always on edge. So how do we counteract these powerful feelings? We need to practice preventative techniques, so we can maintain a calm foundation and better handle stressful situations when they happen. When we are tired or "on" for too long, we are more susceptible to losing the stress battle. Here's what you can do:

1. Get adequate sleep. Take naps (you're not being lazy).

2. Take breaks and give yourself relaxing downtime.

3. Get a massage, meditate, take a bath, or do anything that calms you.

4. Change your physiology by smiling.

Let's say you put those practices to work, but you need some extra support. There are other ways you can inoculate against stress, such as these outlined below.

1. Retrain the negativity bias.

As a result of our evolution we are more likely to focus on the negative than the positive. Neuroscientists have dubbed this the "negativity bias." While this might have helped cavemen stay alive, it adds to our day-to-day stress and overwhelm. So go on a negativity/news fast. Take a break from reading the news, talking to negative people, and watching negative shows and movies. Consciously focus and hold attention on positive things. Try the Three Good Things activity.

2. Know your stress trigger(s).

Different things stress different people out. One minute you're fine, and the next minute you're flipping your lid. This is known as the "amygdala hijack." You've literally lost control of yourself to the most primitive part of your brain. Once you know your triggers, you can be more aware and proactive. List the things that set you off. For each one, list how it might feel like it's threatening your survival. Is it really?

3. Change your mindset and mental conditioning.

Our perception that something is stressful kicks in our stress response. By changing our perception, the same situation can feel less stressful and prevent our stress response. Here's how we can use language to create perception shifts:

Remember, it's (usually) a choice. Most of the things that stress us out are the result of a choice we have made. Remember the choice and why you made it.

Positive self-talk. Studies show that self-talk increases motivation and willingness to endure uncomfortable situations. Self-talk is most effective when it's short, specific, and consistent.

Reframing. Filter out unnecessary negative information; find the silver lining and good in situations and focus on that.

4. Get Social.

Studies have shown that a strong social support network can help build resilience to stress. Having positive, caring people around us can make the hard times seem not so hard. Don't like people or can't see them? Try hanging out with animals for some less complicated love.

5. Get Buddhist.

The understanding that nothing is permanent helps us to not react so strongly to things. So take a deep breath and repeat after me, "This too shall pass."

"OK, all these strategies are great," you're thinking, "but I really don't have the time to implement them. That's why I'm so stressed in the first place!" Here are some quick hits you can employ no matter how busy and stressed you are:

1. Take micro-breaks. If you can't get away for a week or even a day, focus on taking micro-breaks. On the walk between meetings, close your eyes and feel the sun on your face. Focus on and intensify the small moments of relaxation and enjoyment you can get. These micro-breaks add up.

2. Try Chade-Meng Tan's "Joy on Demand" technique. Take three full breaths, in and out. On the first breath, focus on your breath; on the second breath, calm your body; on the third breath, invite joy into your life. Fifteen seconds total time.

3. Practice 4-7-8 Breathing. Breathe in for four seconds, hold your breath for seven seconds, and then slowly exhale for eight seconds.

So take Lil Wayne's advice, be ambitious in your goals, and use the techniques above to better handle the pressures in your life.

Overcome Fear and Performance Anxiety Like a Peak Performer

"If you can love and respect yourself in failure, worlds of adventure and new experiences will open up before you, and your fears will vanish."
—DR. DAVID BURNS, COGNITIVE BEHAVIOR THERAPY PIONEER

In order to take on new challenges and push ourselves past our existing limits, we need to be able to manage fear. If you recall from the chapter on purpose, we learned that the brain assigns meaning to new experiences through our hippocampus comparing the present with the past to determine if it's meaningful or not. But fear works differently.

Thanks to the ground-breaking work of the neuroscientist Joseph LeDoux, we know that when our amygdala determines something to be dangerous, the hippocampus is cut out of the process and the amygdala takes over. This is known as the "amygdala hijack"—what follows is the fight, flight, freeze, or appease responses. As LeDoux points out, when we are scared we are actually hardwired to freeze first. Next we look to run. Only if that is not an option do we fight. And when we believe we are totally outmatched we roll over and play dead. In a performance context, if our amygdala becomes too active we cannot perform in the nuanced ways we need to in order to be successful. Instead, our critical thinking shuts down, all the blood rushes to the large muscles in our bodies so we can run or fight, and our thoughts and behaviors become crude and clumsy. Therefore, when we're doing something that is new and potentially scary to us, we need to keep our prefrontal cortex—the reasoning and rational part of our brain—online and the amygdala subordinate. Now that we understand how fear works, let's look at what we can do to keep ourselves under control while we are working to make breakthroughs in our performance.

I recently started to learn how to ski. At forty-five years old, putting two little slats on my feet and going down an icy mountain really fast certainly gets my amygdala excited. Based on my research, work with clients, and my own experience, here's what I've found most useful in managing fear and performance anxiety:

Connect the activity back to your purpose, and use your purpose to give you the courage to move forward. Courage is not the absence of fear, but rather the drive to move forward even though you are scared. If you can make your motivation, based in your purpose, bigger than your fear, you can keep going.

Make sure what you're doing is in your "proximal zone of learning." This is also known as a "just-right challenge" or "edge." The action is challenging but not so difficult that you can't handle it. Know where your edge is and work just at it or even just inside it.

Narrow your focus and follow the leader. For something that really pushes my fear buttons, like going down a big, icy mountain, if I look at the whole slope, it's just too scary and vast to do on my own. But if I can narrow my focus to the next thing I have to do, I can follow right behind my instructor and follow their lead.

Keep the past in the past. Much of our fear is based on past experiences and not present reality. In my view, the type of fear that ends up impeding our performance, commonly referred to as performance anxiety, is a result of a low-level (or sometimes more significant) trauma.

I am defining trauma as practitioners of EMDR trauma treatment do, which is improperly stored memory. (EMDR stands for "eye movement desensitization and reprocessing"; it's a form of psychotherapy that says that negative thoughts are the result of unprocessed memories.) Essentially, when we are emotionally overwhelmed and our amygdala takes over responding from our hippocampus, which is responsible for storing long-term memory, our brain is not able to recognize an experience that already happened as in the past. Rather, we react as if that thing is happening again now. So when I start to get scared of going downhill and my freeze response begins kicking in, my brain is enacting that time I crashed my bike going down that gnarly hill in college. The more we can become aware of the past experiences that may be creeping into our present performance challenges, the more we can remind ourselves that these were past experiences and are not happening now. For more severe or intractable traumas EMDR treatment might work wonders for you as it has for many others. For that you'll want to seek out a certified provider. And there are EMDR protocols specially designed to enhance performance as well.

Get comfortable with your surroundings. Novelty is one of the main factors that activates our brain's attention. But it can also trigger our fear. Consider the phenomenon known as "the first night effect," in which people do not sleep well during their first night in a new hotel. While consciously they know they are safe, unconsciously this new environment sets off a survival fear in a new and potentially dangerous place. So the more you can do to get comfortable and relaxed in the surroundings where you need to perform, the better. Athletes often have to go to an opposing team's home court to compete. Steph Curry, the all-star basketball player, uses popcorn to make himself more comfortable in away games. A self-professed popcorn addict, when Curry arrives at the stadium he goes to the locker room, puts his stuff down, and heads straight to the popcorn table. And he eats popcorn during and after the game. So think of the things you can do to feel more at home wherever it is you need to perform.

Your body needs to get it. Fear cannot be intellectualized away. Whatever you're doing needs to feel right to you. It's when your nervous system gets that what you're doing is not a cause for alarm, but something you're choosing to do, and then syncs with the activity you are doing. That happens through repetition and those aha moments that can only be experienced. It's a felt sense to look for and try to achieve. Get grounded, feel your feet beneath you, breathe into the activity, and try to feel it. At first it might be short moments, but keep at it and try to hold on to them, and those moments will get longer and longer before the desire to bail takes over. Try hypnotherapy and/or somatic experiencing for interventions that work on the subconscious and physiological levels in order to overcome fear.

Getting past yourself. So often, our fear has to do with an over-focus on ourselves and how we might get hurt or be negatively impacted. The more we can open up this narrow perspective to see the bigger picture, the more supported we can feel. One way to do this is to focus on helping others during the activity we are doing. When I began to support other participants in my ski lessons, I forgot about my own fears.

Love and respect yourself. As the quote from Dr. David Burns says, we need to have a healthy love and respect for ourselves. Knowing that we are doing our best, are being compassionate with ourselves, and will be there to take care of ourselves helps to calm the nervous system. Fear doesn't quite vanish, as Dr. Burns says, but it can take the edge off.

The last essential component of becoming a peak performer makes everything in this chapter easier and faster to implement. Yet, people come up with all kinds of reasons and excuses not to do it. The next section debunks these excuses and shows you how to implement this last key piece.

BE ELITE: BUILD YOUR PERSONAL TEAM LIKE A PEAK PERFORMER

I grew up playing tennis and still follow it. In the past, players used to have one coach at most. Today they are assembling larger and more varied support teams to help them in their quest to be the best they can be. Novak Djokovic, who is closing in fast on being considered the GOAT (greatest of all time), is known for the significance of his team. Top players often employ a coach, fitness trainer, physiotherapist, massage therapist, acupuncturist, chiropractor, nutritionist, chef, and whomever else they believe they need to excel.

These are people who have expertise in specific areas that are important for players to perform their best. They provide motivation, develop training and recovery programs, deliver informed feedback so players can make important changes, and help them recover more quickly when they get injured—all toward the end of helping them reach their goals and meet their potential.

So why don't we all assemble teams of experts, a personal support team if you will, to help us make progress in the areas of life that are most important to us? In my work as a performance coach and psychotherapist I see three common misassumptions that stop people from getting themselves the help they need to be their best.

1. "Getting help means I am weak or deficient."

Some people are afraid that getting help acknowledges some kind of weakness, and this insecurity is incredibly undermining to peak performance. No matter how good you are, you can still do better. Certain kinds of support in particular have been stigmatized in our culture—therapy is a prime example and, to a lesser but similar extent, coaching. The former Google and Alphabet CEO, Eric Schmidt, reflects on the suggestion that he get an executive coach:

"I initially resented the advice, because after all, I was a CEO. I was pretty experienced. Why would I need a coach? Am I doing something wrong? My argument was, how could a coach advise me if I'm the best person in the world at this? But that's not what a coach does. The coach doesn't have to play the sport as well as you do. They have to watch you and get you to be your best."

The notion of coaching seems to be gaining acceptance in the tech world, where more and more CEOs are seeing that it can give them a helpful edge. Having people help you does not mean you are weak or deficient. It means you are smart and willing to do what it takes to achieve your goals.

2. "I don't want to spend the money."

Some people are open to help but do not want to spend the money. I am consistently surprised that people are willing to spend money on almost everything but their personal development. Spending money in this way is an investment in ourselves and will pay dividends tenfold. We must invest in ourselves. Your personal team does not have to cost you an arm and a leg. It is possible to find quality people and not break the bank as long as you're OK with these folks not being on your full-time payroll or traveling with you on your business trips.

3. "I can do it myself."

Some believe they can do it on their own. If you think about this from the perspective of an athlete, this notion is fairly ridiculous. You cannot see yourself in ways that others can, and you cannot possibly be an expert in every area that is important for your overall success. The truth is, most of us have never thought about ourselves as elite performers with specific activities in which we want to excel, much less someone who warrants having a team of people helping us be our best. But in fact, we can put together our own roster to help us be our best.

What follows are some areas and recommendations you might consider in building your personal team. (Note: I do think that real people will be most effective for building your team in the areas you want to grow in, but I recognize that cost, preference, and ease may make it sensible to use an app for support, so I've tried to recommend some quality ones here as well.)

If health and fitness are important to you . . . Consider getting a trainer (whom you can find at your local gym) or a nutritionist (some medical plans will cover this). You can also make some smaller investments, such as getting a massage once a month. App suggestions: NYTimes 7 Minute Workout, Strava, My Fitness Pal

If your mental health and happiness are important to you . . . Consider getting a therapist. If you already have a therapist and are seeking more ways to emphasize this, then consider taking courses in mindfulness, yoga, or art. App suggestions: Talk Space, Headspace, 10% Happier

If your work and professional development are important to you . . . Consider getting an executive coach. Your company may offer coaching or may reimburse you as part of your professional development allotment. Coaching can be done in-person or via phone or video conference. App suggestion: There are some attempts underway to scale coaching with technology, but I'm not sure there's a replacement for having someone who gets to know you (warts and all) and can give you real, honest, and caring feedback for your growth. But if you're interested you can check out Better Up.

If your relationship is important to you and needs work . . . Consider a couples counselor. Don't be afraid to enter the self-help section of the bookstore and read well-received books like *Getting the Love You Want,* by Harville Hendrix, and use an author's expertise to help you and your partner grow for each other.

If being a great parent is important to you . . . Seek out a child and adolescent psychologist. If you travel a lot and want to still read aloud to your child, consider an app like Kindoma that aims to close the gap.

If your wealth is important to you . . . Consider adding a financial planner or a good real estate broker to your life team. You can also seek out a variety of financial management services or apps, such as Mint or You Need a Budget.

Start Building Your Team

The first step to building a team that will help you succeed is getting clear about where you want or need to make progress. Take some time to think about your values and what in your life is most important for you to get better and succeed at. Next, find yourself an expert in each of those areas (ask your friends for referrals to find the right people). Develop a relationship with that person, so they get to know you and how to best help you. Work with that person to reach your goals. Go to that person when you need support. Change that person if it's not working or you need something different. You don't need to be an elite athlete to build your personal team. As Bill Gates says, "Everyone needs a coach." So who do you need on your team?

Congratulations, you now have all the tools you need to become a peak performer. Put them into use and continue honing them, and there will be no stopping you from being your best.

YOUR TURN—WHOLE-SELF EXERCISE

The following exercises will help you identify, get back in touch with, and start to reactivate key parts of yourself, allowing you to reclaim your whole self. Let's do some gardening!

STEP 1: PREPARING THE SOIL: "WHOLE-SELF AUDIT"

Below are common aspects of self that can go underdeveloped. Give each trait below a score on a scale of 1–10 in terms of how much you are currently able to express this aspect of yourself.

Being aggressive _____

Being in charge _____

Being loving _____

Being affectionate _____

Being tender _____

Being imperfect _____

Failing _____

Being incompetent _____

Being silly _____

Having fun _____

Being joyful _____

Being carefree _____

Relaxing _____

Being creative _____

Being artistic _____

Being physical _____

Being strong _____

Being athletic _____

Being successful _____

Making money _____

Next, answer these questions:

What would my partner or a close friend say is missing with me?

"So and so is great, but they are not . . ."

What kind of people do I admire or wish I were more like?

Whom do I find myself being jealous of?

What did I see a lot at home and what didn't I see at home very often?

Which attributes above are most holding me back from being more successful in an important area of my life right now?

STEP 2: PLANTING THE SEEDS

For each aspect that you scored less than a 7 in the Whole-Self Audit, describe what it would give you if you started seeing yourself as that kind of person and expressed more of that trait? (Example: Seeing myself as an affectionate person would bring more tenderness and joy into my life. It would reduce stress. Being more affectionate would let my partner know I love her and would open the door to her being more affectionate to me, which would help me know she loves me.)

STEP 3: GIVING WATER AND LIGHT

Choose three to five attributes from the exercises above that, if you really nurtured in yourself, would make the biggest difference in your life right now, personally and professionally. For each write down at least one thing you will commit to doing every day to cultivate that trait. (Example: To become more affectionate, I will hug my wife every day for a little bit longer than is comfortable for me. I will let my wife know that this is something I'm working on and would like her support with.)

STEP 4: WATCH YOURSELF GROW

At first, you might not see much progress or it will feel foreign and uncomfortable to bring these aspects of yourself into being. People you know might look at you funny and wonder what is going on. But with continued effort, expression, and patience you will begin to see these parts of yourself grow, and you will feel yourself shift to accommodate them as they take their rightful place within you. Feel free to take the Whole-Self Audit again in six months or a year to see what has changed and what you might want to plant next in the garden as you continue to cultivate your whole self and your full potential.

Exercise: Transforming Limiting Beliefs

PART 1: IDENTIFYING THE IMPOSTER

What was a recent situation where you doubted yourself, felt you were not good enough or didn't belong? (For example, at a recent executive team meeting I didn't offer my opinion because I felt that my idea would be judged as naïve.)

What assumption(s) about yourself are you making? (For example, I'm assuming that because I am the youngest member of the Executive Team I have the least experience, my ideas are not as good as others', and I don't really belong on this team.)

What is the underlying belief driving these assumptions? (For example, that I'm not enough.)

What are the origins of this belief? (For example, as the youngest child I always felt that my older siblings were better than I was at everything.)

What triggers this belief now? When does it show up? (For example, when I'm in a group that feels competitive I start to shut down and defer to others who I feel have more experience or are smarter than I am.)

How is this belief holding me back? (For example, it prevents me from confidently speaking up and contributing what I have to offer. It may be preventing me from getting a promotion.)

PART 2: CREATING A NEW BELIEF

When confronted with a similar situation where I've doubted myself, what new, different assumptions would I like to have about myself? (For example, I know I am smart and hardworking, my ideas are good, and I do belong on this team. In fact, my youth offers a unique perspective that others don't have.)

What underlying new belief would drive these new assumptions above? (For example, I am enough.)

Who can be a role model for your new belief? (This can be someone you know personally or know of. For example, the current prime minister of New Zealand, Jacinda Ardern, who became the youngest female head of government at thirty-seven years old.)

PART 3: CONSOLIDATING THE NEW BELIEF

If I knew (the opposite of the self-limiting belief) was true I would . . . (For example, if I knew I was enough, I would start speaking up at Executive Team meetings more confidently.)

I'm ready for a bigger step in the direction of my new belief. It is . . . (For example, I'm going to do a Ted Talk this year and not wait until I have enough experience to belong as a Ted speaker.)

Some steps I can begin taking now using my new belief are . . . (For example, I'm going to volunteer to present at the next executive team meeting and I'm going to register to speak and put together my deck for the conference next month.)

When the self-doubt begins I will use the following positive self-talk and reframing techniques to reinforce my new belief . . . (For example, "I am enough"; "Hard work will pay off"; "My perspective is unique because I am young"; and "If Jacinda can do it, so can I.")

Congratulations, you have transformed your Imposter!

CHAPTER SIX

Peak Performance Parenting

The next chapters look at how to put the Peak Performance Formula into practice. The three areas of parenting, teams, and organizations are where many of us spend significant parts of our lives aspiring to be our best.

BLAKE MYCOSKIE, FOUNDER, TOM'S SHOES

Put family first

Blake Mycoskie is the founder of Tom's Shoes. Chances are you have a pair of Tom's in your shoe rack. After traveling to poor areas in Argentina in 2006 with a group that provided shoes to poor children, Blake founded a shoe company that would both generate profit and help poor children worldwide. He is credited with creating and popularizing the "one for one" business model in which a pair of shoes would be donated for every pair bought. But I'm not here to tell you about Blake's big heart or business prowess. Blake is a peak performance parent. How do I know this? An Instagram post on April 7, 2020, at the beginning of the COVID-19 pandemic caught my eye. Here's the post:

> "5 years ago when we had our son, my (now ex-wife/friend/ co-parent) and i wrote these family values together. We had a lot of time on our hands because i was taking a few months off of work for paternity leave and we were able to really contemplate what words would guide the 'culture' of our new family, just like a mission statement and values guide a company. To this day, these values guide us. During this time, i highly recommend all families (and singles) take the time to think about their mission statement and core values and then display them prominently in your home (mine is in the kitchen and I print them on t shirts i give to guests who visit). And have these values guide you and as you come out of this experience stronger and more clear on how you and your family will move in this new world."

He included a photo of his family mission and core values written in marker on a flip chart. Here they are:

Mission: To live courageous lives, with grace and moderation

Core Values:

1. Put family first
2. Be present

3. Give generously

4. Love ourselves, others, and the planet

5. Invest in personal growth

6. Be curious

7. Make time for play

With the exception of replacing "mission" with "purpose" and reducing the core values from seven to four, Blake nails the concept of applying purpose and values to creating a family culture and becoming a more intentional and effective parent.

Indra Nooyi, the former CEO of PepsiCo, tells the story of finding out she was going to be named head of Pepsi, going home to share the news with her family, and being told by her mother to go out and buy milk. According to Nooyi, women can't have it all. They cannot be high-powered businesspeople and high-performing moms. Being a parent has long been viewed as an impediment to peak performance, let alone something to be a peak performer at. This is changing. The number of elite performers who are having kids while staying at the top of their game seems to be increasing. And not just having kids, but embracing the identity of being proud parents in addition to their identity as elite performers.

Jacinda Ardern, the prime minister of New Zealand, had a baby while in office. Tennis legends Serena Williams, Roger Federer, and Novak Djokovic, as well as basketball greats LeBron James and Steph Curry, are just a few examples of proud parents who remain at the very top of their sports. And for many, like the professional golfer Charley Hoffman, parenthood has provided both renewed motivation to achieve as well as perspective on life in the face of setback and loss.

BECOME A PEAK PERFORMING PARENT

While we can find numerous examples of people incorporating parenting into their pursuit of peak performance in athletics and work, what is lacking is the application of peak performance principles to parenting itself. Peak performers like to excel at whatever they do. And since parenting is such a vital job it is the focus of this chapter. The first step toward becoming a peak performing parent is to grow up yourself. Here's how.

Heal Your Inner Child

Sleep deprived, not performing at the top of your game at work, and not feeling or looking your best physically—it almost feels as if your life as you've known it is over. And it is. As much as you may be tempted to count the years until things go back to normal, and even though things do get easier and you do get some time back, the truth is that this is the new normal. You are now a parent, and your identity is inextricably linked with raising kids.

You need time with your kids, time to work, time to take care of things at home (which now that you have kids becomes a lot more), time to make sure your relationship is intact (which now that you have kids comes under increasing strain), and then whatever remaining time there is (which is very little) can be for you.

As happy as I was with my family and my role as a dad, and as much as I committed to it, I was also vaguely aware of a kind of yearning for something for myself that caused a sense of dissatisfaction with it all. And I couldn't really put my finger on what I was yearning for until one day I figured it out: I was yearning for what was incomplete about my relationship with my own father—that in some way what I didn't get the child inside me was still hopeful he would get someday. Now, being a dad was like almost guaranteeing I would never get it. The truth is, we are all used to being taken care of—by our parents, the people we date, our spouses. We are also used to being the center of our worlds, thinking mostly about ourselves and expecting others to do so as well. Then you become a parent and become the caregiver. Baby becomes the center of attention, and the needs of the parents take a backseat.

But having kids is an incredible opportunity to give as a parent what you never got from your own parents. And in doing so to have the experience of having what you most yearn for, this time as a parent rather than as a child and giving this gift to your child. The satisfaction comes in knowing that in giving to your child what you yourself didn't get, you are also healing the child in you that has gone without all these years. Don't just give this to your child, but be that person for everyone in your life. Follow these steps to heal your inner child and make sure you get what you need now.

Get in touch with the experience you had with your own parents and with what was incomplete for you (i.e., what you did not get). And what you might be repeating from your parents, which you didn't want to do with your child. Consciously stop repeating what you didn't want from your parents and start giving to your child— and heal yourself in the process.

Embrace being a parent instead of fighting it. As a friend of mine says, "It's not messing up your flow, it is your flow." Reorient your life around helping this young person grow and develop. Become a bit of a kid again and relive some of the joy of these first experiences through their eyes.

Find other parents with kids your kid's age. Hang out with them and enjoy the camaraderie that disappears when you don't have time (or energy) to hang with friends anymore.

Make that time for yourself count. Be sure to do something that really fulfills and energizes you. And give that to your partner.

Now let's use the Peak Performance Formula to take our parenting to the next level.

Create a Family Purpose Statement

Like your individual purpose, the family purpose statement gets to the essence of who you are and what you believe, but now as a family. It answers the question of "Why do we exist as a family?" I'm pretty sure the answer is not "to get the kids to school on time, be stressed out about money, and deprive ourselves of sleep." There is a deeper reason you had a family. The purpose statement reminds you of the aspirations you have for your family.

Define Your Family Values

Remember, core values change depending on the context. So as a parent you should have a unique set of values that will guide your behavior to specifically be the kind of parent you strive to be. You can have a set of core values for yourself as well as for your family.

Given the kind of dad I want to be for my kids, my core values are:

Patience. Let things roll off my back; remember that it's not that big a deal; take deep breaths and smile; stop being in a rush.

Playfulness. Make things fun/into games; keep a positive perspective; encourage our passions.

Be loving. Be affectionate; say "I love you"; listen well; have their best interests at heart.

Make it easy. Make sure everyone's needs are being met; limit transitions; keep stress low.

Here's the purpose statement and core values for my family:

Form a Family Vision

The family vision can start with your own single vision for the kind of family life you want to create. But the more it can be a joint vision with your partner and with your kids as they get old enough, the more it will become a true family vision that incorporates what every member of the family would like to manifest. The vision should include what you would like things to look like with your significant other, where you live, what you do for fun as a family, and any other details that are important for you.

BETTER AT WHAT? HELPING OUR KIDS EXCEL (AND BE HAPPY)

As we support our kids in being their best, it's important that we don't end up stifling them in the process. A major tenet of therapy and coaching is that we do not impose our wants and desires onto our clients. Instead, we listen and watch carefully as we try to attune to what they really yearn for. In the same way, peak performance parenting involves helping our kids figure out for themselves what they love; what their purpose, values, and vision are; and then we try to support them as best we can to be that best version of themselves. In addition to coming up with a family purpose, values, and vision (which ideally includes input from your kids if they're old enough), here's what we can do to help support the development of our kids instead of imposing our own deferred dreams on them:

Instead of pushing them into what you want them to be good at, expose your kids to a lot of things and follow their lead for what they like and want to pursue further.

Use a growth mindset focusing on the process instead of the results. Praise effort and ingenuity instead of praising being "good" or winning.

Be there for them when things don't go well and they have a setback. If they want to quit, remind them of the commitment they made and that they can decide to stop once the commitment is over (e.g., once the sporting season ends).

Connect and have fun with them. More than anything else this will foster their joy for whatever they do.

Love them unconditionally. The core belief they will form about themselves when they know they are fundamentally worthy and loved will give them the confidence they need to succesfully navigate whatever challenges life throws at them.

So apply the same concepts to your family that individual peak performers, teams, and companies use to ensure that they have clarity around who they are, how they do what they do, and what they want to achieve.

YOUR TURN—DEFINE YOUR FAMILY VALUES

In order to create your own family values, follow these steps:

1. Interview people who know your family well in order to draw out what is essential about you. Ask them questions like, "What three words would you use to describe us as a family?" and "What is most special or unique about us as a family?"

2. Get together as a family to devise a family purpose statement and ascertain core guiding values that are most important for you all. Get things started by asking everyone, "What is one thing you are most proud of about our family?" and "When friends come over, what experience do we want them to have?" Next, list ten values that are important to your family and circle the four that are most important.

3. Develop norms, rituals, and visual cues based on your family's purpose and values. (Do you wear shoes in the house? Do you eat dinner together every night? Do you serve food in a soup kitchen on Thanksgiving? Do you have quotes hanging around the house? These are examples of norms, rituals, and cues.)

4. Make a Family Values plaque that you can hang on your wall to help keep your values front and center in your home.

CHAPTER SEVEN

Peak Performance Leaders

VICKI KNOTT, CEO AND COFOUNDER, CRUX OCM

Simplifying the energy industry

We all have an essence to who we are, otherwise known as our purpose. The more we know that essence and do work that is aligned to it, the more effective and fulfilled we will be. Vicki Knott is drawn to simplicity. As a young child, she loved playing with rocks in her parents' fishing cottage. She has always loved breaking things down and making them easier. Her purpose in life is to simplify complexity. So it's no surprise the company she cofounded and is CEO of, Crux, seeks to simplify one of the most complex and entrenched industries on the planet. As she describes, "The oil and gas industry is conservative and old-school, stuck in their ways, and one of the most adverse industries to change."

Vicki trained as a control room operator and worked in oil and gas both in the field and with industry regulators. She saw first-hand how the increasing complexity of control room operations was causing operator fatigue, which could lead to errors with big implications. "Operators are the front line to profits and losses, safety, and environmental hazards," Vicki explains. "Similar to an airplane pilot, control room operators control the oil and gas assets that provide the world its energy."

So "how can we reduce complexity and control room operator workload?" That was the question that prompted her to found her company. Crux provides automation and software innovation to control room operations with the goal of improving efficiency, safety, and overall economics in the energy industry. Crux's vision is to become the global default autopilot software for control rooms. "I want to completely reengineer industrial control systems," Vicki beams. "I mean, why can't a control room operator have the proper automation and security to operate an entire gas facility from anywhere they want via a tablet or computer?" That's a pretty bold vision for someone who got their start playing with rocks. How will she make it a reality?

Early on in my coaching work with Vicki, we developed her "leadership persona," a blueprint of her most authentic and effective leadership style. The leadership persona helped her articulate her purpose and leadership core values, identify leaders she wants to emulate, and flaws to avoid projecting into her company, as well as practices to sustain her energy.

When she first started on her leadership journey, Vicki defaulted to the people she thought she should be idolizing and emulating. For her those were scientists. But these weren't the people who really exemplified who she was or wanted to be as a leader. "What feels good and right and gets me excited are actually Taylor Swift and Harley Quinn. Taylor is an entrepreneurial genius, and nice. Harley Quinn is a complete train wreck, and sometimes I need to channel that to get things done."

Vicki's core values help ensure she's building a company she loves and can bring her vision to life. "These values make the company a place I want to be." After brainstorming a list of ten important guiding principles to be successful, she selected the four most important to her success. Vicki's core leadership values are: 1) be inclusive, 2) work smart and be accountable, 3) show confident decisiveness with transparency, and 4) have fun. Along with her leadership core values, Vicki has photos of Taylor Swift and Harley Quinn at the ready to remind her of who she is, in essence, as a leader.

Founding a company is hard work. Raising millions of dollars, hiring an effective team, creating technically complex products, and scaling a company all to disrupt an incredibly entrenched industry takes fortitude and endurance. To handle it, Vicki makes sure she gets eight to nine hours of sleep per night, meditates daily, exercises three to four times per week, eats a mostly vegan diet, does lots of outdoor activities, and cuddles her two cats often. These self-care and energy management practices help ensure her long-term performance and well-being. With a clearer understanding of who she is as a leader and what will allow her to be most effective, Vicki and Crux are poised to make an incredible impact on the world.

Much has been written about leadership, some of it actually good, and I don't want to give a broad survey of leadership theory. But I do want to share how utilizing purpose, values, and vision along with the go-to tools of peak performers can help you become a more effective and happier leader for a longer time. Leaders inherently try to influence others and provide direction and order to those in our charge. It is a big responsibility to be looked to and counted on in this way, and to do right by those who have agreed to follow us. So we need to make sure we are cultivating the best version of ourselves to lead. Here's what that looks like.

WHAT'S THE PROBLEM?

According to Dr. Ron Heifetz, the founding director of the Center for Public Leadership at Harvard University, purpose, at its core, asks and answers the question "What's the problem you are trying to solve?" Heifetz defines *problem* as, "the gap between the current reality and what we aspire to." Heifetz argues that much of the theory on leadership focuses on personal capacity and the tools or competencies that create more effective leaders. Attributes such as charisma, composure, decisiveness, and persuasiveness are important, but they lack something. As Heifetz explains, "What really differentiates a carpenter from a surgeon is not the tools they use, but the problems they are trying to solve." And often it's not exactly clear what the problem is or what our aspirations should be. Figuring out and getting people to agree on the problem that needs solving is a central task of leadership. And these problems often come with conflicting sets of values that we must work to figure out, which should be superior and which are subsidiary. These values often come with the baggage and immovability of our traditions, whether they be religious, cultural, or familial.

By getting clear on the problem we are trying to solve, which values are most important, and the creative ways to honor multiple values and then facilitating this clarity in others, we can be more effective and successful leaders. (To learn more about Heifetz's theory and practice of leadership I highly recommend his books, *Leadership without Easy Answers* and *Leadership on the Line*.)

Don't Project Your Flaws

As the venture investor Ben Horowitz says, leaders program their own flaws into the culture of their organizations. When he was a CEO, his tendency to get lost in the details of things showed up in the company as meetings with no agendas that consistently ran over schedule. Leaders bring their own psychologies into the organizations they lead. This is important on two levels. First, as the example above illustrates, when a leader places his or her own shortcomings into the whole organization, inefficiencies and dysfunction are created. Second, and perhaps more important, when through a process known as projection, leaders put that which they can least stand in themselves into their organizations and are forced to face it daily, work becomes a veritable second circle of hell for them. Working with founders and CEOs, I've seen this many times. In an act of unconscious masochism, it causes tremendous suffering to leaders who end up creating the worst job possible for themselves. And employees go nuts, because these traits that are unacceptable to the leader become red herrings, and the culture police are on high alert to put a stop to it.

This psychological process called projection is the disavowal of unacceptable traits or qualities and the attribution of them to others. Here are two fairly common examples:

Leaders who cannot tolerate making mistakes—because they always had to be perfect for their parents—disavow imperfection, see it everywhere in their employees' work, and disdain it. Of course, some employees' insecurities about being inadequate, which stem from their own upbringing, get activated and they begin to enact their own set of responses to protect themselves psychologically. Perhaps they work even harder to please their boss, blame others for the substandard results, or go home and eat a tub of ice cream and sink into depression. Mistakes are a part of life. In addition to making everyone anxious and on edge this dynamic actually hurts the organization as learning from mistakes rather than avoiding or punishing them is how we actually get better.

Leaders who are anti-authority. They never liked being told what to do, and this is one reason they started their own company or aspired to a leadership position where they get to call the shots. But because they can't tolerate being told what to do, they also can't stand being challenged. They don't understand why their employees can't seem to follow directions, and they see everyone as insubordinate. And again, employees who grew up with issues around authoritarian figures will enact their own set of counterproductive responses to deal with the boss who comes across as the tyrant they grew up with at home. We all know that great leaders must be open to hearing what's not working.

Leaders need to be self-aware of the things they cannot tolerate in themselves and thereby are at risk of projecting. For these they must create safeguards against letting their organizations be the container for their projections. Being a leader is about taking responsibility for our organizations and the people in them. This needs to start with owning the parts of ourselves that we most dislike or find most abhorrent. As uncomfortable as this may be it's critical to our success and fulfillment as leaders. One way to become more self-aware and intentional as a leader is through the cultivation of a leadership persona. Here's what it is and why you need one.

Create Your Leadership Persona

In the 1950s and '60s, one of the most popular courses among business students at Berkeley and the University of Pennsylvania was actually an anthropology and sociology class, taught by a professor named

Erving Goffman. Why were throngs of business students clamoring to enroll in this course?

Let's start with the professor. Erving Goffman is widely considered one of the most influential sociologists of the twentieth century, and he made his mark with his first book, now a classic in that field, called *The Presentation of Self in Everyday Life*. In this book, Goffman describes how all actions are social performances that aim to convey and maintain impressions of oneself to others. We are, in essence, actors on a stage, performing to an audience. We play different roles depending on the audience—our friends, our family, our colleagues, our supervisors, etc. And we employ varied and different techniques in order to successfully sustain our performance to our given audience. Goffman refers to these roles as "personas" (derived from the Latin reference to a theatrical mask), which are composed of the combination of techniques we use to effectively perform.

Although these roles are all "you," they are and should be different given the context. By being intentional and self-aware about our personas, we can ensure that we are showing up in a way that is both optimally effective given the role we are in and authentic to who we are. So those hundreds of business students were coming to learn how to construct their most effective role for success in their careers—as well as gain an advantage over those who weren't doing so.

When I founded and led my first organization, I had many conflicting and often cliché ideas of what an effective "leader" was. I had read a lot of leadership theory and seen a lot of movies. When it came to my own leadership opportunity, I thought I had to work myself to exhaustion, be "the first one there and last one to leave." I thought I had to gain consensus for every decision. I thought I had to be Mel Gibson in *Braveheart* and make passionate speeches before going into daily battle. I often felt inauthentic, ineffective, and wiped out from trying to be all things to all people. And because I didn't really know who I was as the leader of this organization, I think my employees were often confused about what I was communicating to them, since they were experiencing conflicting "greatest hits" styles of others' leadership roles. This was because I lacked my own leadership persona.

A "leadership persona" is the intentional role we play as someone leading a team, an organization, or any effort that requires us to mobilize others for a common goal. It asks us to define ourselves as a leader, to think about qualities we most admire in other leaders as well as those we most admire about ourselves. It includes connecting our personal purpose to our leadership role and the essential values that will successfully guide us to success in that role. It asks us to consider the type and quality of relationships we have with those we work with, the behaviors we will strive to model for our teams, how we will make decisions and give feedback, the ways in which we will manage work-life balance, and how we will respond in the most challenging leadership situations. It even asks us to consider how we will dress (i.e., what costume, literally, we will wear for our leadership performance).

I work with leaders to reflect on and address these key components of who they are and really want to be as a leader. And I have found, time and again, the result of designing a leadership persona is a happier, more authentic, more sustainable, and ultimately more effective leader.

YOUR TURN—CREATE YOUR LEADERSHIP PERSONA

A persona is an aspect of one's character that is presented to and perceived by others. We assume different personas, depending on the role we are playing (e.g., friend, son/daughter, parent, leader, etc.). Although these roles are all "you," they are and should be different. By being intentional about our personas, we can ensure we are showing up in a way that is both optimally effective given the role we are in and authentic to who we are. To hone your leadership persona, answer the following questions:

Think of a time when you were being most effective and authentic as a leader. When was it and what traits were you exhibiting?

Who are your heroes? What do you admire most about them?

How do you want people to describe you as a leader? When you're gone, how do you want to be remembered?

Leadership Core Values: What are the essential behaviors that will define your success as a leader?

Leadership Purpose Statement: Why do you get out of bed in the morning?

Describe the nature of the relationships you want to have at work.

How do you want to give feedback?

How do you want to make decisions?

What actions, behaviors, ways of being do you model for your team?

How do you think about balancing work-life? And how do you practice self-care?

What kind of public speaker do you want to be? What do you need to do to get better at this?

What kind of appearance is most consistent with your persona (e.g., dress, grooming, etc.)?

What flaws do you have that you do not want to bring into your organization? What safeguards can you institute?

What is one thing that can quickly connect you to or remind you of your leadership persona?

CHAPTER EIGHT

Peak Performance Organizations

JACK HEATH, MENTAL HEALTH LEADER

An egoless culture

In 1992, Jack Heath's cousin took his own life. At the time, Jack had been mounting a climb to the top of Australia's political class, first working as a speechwriter and adviser to the foreign and trade ministers, and then as a senior adviser to the Australian prime minister. Then, in 1994, Jack's daughter was born six weeks premature, his parents were divorcing, and he had developed chronic fatigue from working too much. Feeling that he needed a break, Jack enrolled in a ten-day Tibetan Buddhist meditation course. During this retreat, he came to the realization that he had to stop the work he was doing. His political climb to the top was successful but not sustainable.

When Jack returned from his retreat, he handed in his resignation to the prime minister. Jack remembered his cousin and began to feel a strong impulse to do something about the rising youth suicide rates in Australia at the time. Jack reached out to the head of Microsoft Australia, whom he'd gotten to know through his work at the prime minister's office, and together they launched Inspire in 1996.

Inspire is an Australian-based nonprofit whose mission is to create opportunities for young people aged sixteen to twenty-five to change their world. Thanks in part to Inspire, youth suicide rates had fallen a remarkable 47 percent in Australia at the time of our conversation.

Jack shared his leadership philosophy of doing the right thing in the right way. "The challenge is to grow Inspire from a position of genuine compassion and concern, not from the adrenaline, excitement, and euphoria of being entrepreneurial. The ego is always getting in the way of selfless service."

Jack's not sure that he's mastered his ego yet, but he's aware of it. At Inspire, employees were given an extra week off specifically as a time to reflect. "We ask everyone to check their motivation to make sure it's right. With a clear mind we have greater impact. Intention is like nuclear power; if it's not right it can be very dangerous." Jack advises that everyone find a way to find time to reflect in his or her own life.

Jack's motto for Inspire was to keep your heart warm, head cool, and ears open. "Having a warm heart means you are compassionate. Head cool means that you think things through and do not act out of anger. Ears open means you listen to people and hear what they are saying, even if it's something you don't want to hear." This, he says, will bring the right motivation that can overcome the ego.

Jack and Inspire offer a great example of how a leader getting clear on their personal purpose, values, and vision and then creating a culture with clear organizational purpose, values, and vision can lead to amazing results. Jack continues his work to improve the lives of Australians affected by mental illness as the CEO of Sane. Learn more about Sane's work at https://www.sane.org/.

What allows some organizations to continually outperform their peers year over year for decades? Some will argue they have a superior product. Some will argue they have the best and brightest leadership or employees. These may be true. But what enables these to be true lies in the culture of the organization.

Recently there has been a lot of focus on organizational culture in the news, and what can happen when culture goes bad. Uber is possibly permanently tarnished by the problematic leadership and workplace culture it was built on. And by now we've all read about the leadership and culture fiasco at WeWork, which helped derail its IPO and caused its valuation to plunge by more than 80 percent. Even if your organization isn't a high-profile tech giant or hasn't made the news for its toxic work environment, culture is a powerful force that shapes the day-to-day behaviors of employees and outcomes of organizations in all industries of all sizes. I have learned through my own experience founding and leading an organization and working with founders and CEOs that more than anything else, culture is what really drives outcomes. And lo and behold, the key building blocks of an organization's culture are its purpose, values, and vision (aka the Peak Performance Formula).

CULTURE STARTS AT THE TOP

Of course, company culture starts with the organization's leadership. People look to the leadership for an indication of which behaviors are expected and which are not. If the leader cannot clearly articulate the vision and the leadership team lacks cohesion, then meetings start late, agendas are not set, and the staff gets the message that these things don't matter and that there's nothing unifying the team. What results is an every-person-for-themselves environment where people lack a sense of purpose, are unhappy, and feel unsafe. Even the people who support the leadership are neutralized when there are no explicit norms of behavior, since there is nothing to hold colleagues accountable to or offer support for.

Organizations Need Purpose

Because people want purpose in their lives, organizations need to demonstrate a clear sense of purpose to help employees find the work meaningful and worth showing up for. If they fail to, as the poet and leadership consultant David Whyte writes, "Young spirits can shrivel and die on contact when ambushed by the orphaned and disowned shadows of many corporate cultures."

Values Are the Drivers of Culture

Culture is not ping-pong and bean bags. Culture is really made up of purpose (why the organization exists) and values (the key behaviors that create a sense of shared expectation and accountability in any organization). These behaviors become embedded through norms and rituals, which are established and reinforced. A norm that underscores the value of being present could be giving full attention to each other at staff meetings (i.e., not reading emails or checking phones). A ritual to reinforce a value of being collaborative could be a stand-up meeting every Monday where staff share what they are working on and what support they need from each other.

Vision Creates Striving and Direction

Vision is both aspirational and ultimately achievable. It provides everyone in the organization a direction to push toward and something to strive for. This is where good strategic planning comes in, along with clear communication of a compelling vision to everyone in the organization.

Culture Eats Strategy for Breakfast

There's a saying: "Culture eats strategy for breakfast." You can have the best strategic plan in the world, but if the people in your organization can't execute, your strategy is worth about as much as the paper it's written on. If, however, you believe that the people in your organization are the single most important driver of outcomes, then your organizational culture is something you need to pay close attention to.

Founders of organizations often neglect the critical work of building great cultures. One reason for this is that founders typically have great technical expertise (perhaps they were former teachers who want to start a school or software engineers launching a technology company). And while they are brilliant educators or developers, they haven't managed people or built organizations before. And in the throes of start-up with so much to focus on it's easy to lose sight of what will really drive outcomes, the people in the organization.

The Chicken or the Egg Question of "Culture"

"But we have a clear mission and we hire really smart people," many leaders believe, "so it follows that they will figure out how to work together to achieve our collective goals, right?" Here's the thing: culture will be formed in any organization. The question is whether it will be left to chance or intentionally designed to point everyone in the direction you want to go and bring out the best in people.

Some indications that a culture is weak include poor staff attendance, high turnover, lots of negative watercooler talk, and the organization not getting the results it wants. Conversely, organizations with strong cultures are places people enjoy going to every day, where they stay to build their careers, and where ideas and initiatives about how to drive growth come from engaged employees.

Core values are not just words on a company's website. To be effective, they should be created with those who are expected to uphold them, and they must be imbued with real meaning to those particular people, i.e., they should not be taken from another organization or developed by the leadership and given to the staff. These will be empty words on a page.

Don't Impose Culture

A word of caution: it's a fine line between building culture and imposing it on people. It's one thing to do exercises together as a team to build cultural values, and it's another thing to hand employees a piece of paper and say, "This is what matters to us, this is how we show we're positive."

Engage them in a process to create culture together, get their input, and reflect their ideas back to them. This will create not just buy-in, but true investment when they see their thinking reflected in the values and rituals they are being asked to uphold.

When there is a strong, positive culture with clear purpose, values, and vision staff can support one another and hold each other accountable to uphold the behaviors that are important to the organization and its people.

YOUR TURN—CREATE A CULTURE GUIDE

Regardless of whether you are a leader or member of an organization, a department, or your kid's Little League team you can help to ensure a strong culture is created and maintained. Here's how:

1. Enact a process to unearth the values that matter most to the group's health and success. One great question to get the ball rolling is to ask each team member, "What is one thing in our culture you are really proud of?"

2. Based on those values, agree on the norms and rituals that all team members will uphold. Dedicate time to establishing these norms and rituals, and designate time throughout the year to reinforce the culture.

3. Build the team with culture in mind. Design a process that screens for and makes clear to prospective team members what core values they will be expected to live by.

4. Create a culture guide that articulates the purpose, core values, norms, and rituals that define your culture. Use this guide in interviewing and hiring, onboarding, performance reviews, and for promotion and compensation decisions.

CHAPTER NINE

Peak Performance in Times of Crisis

PRESTON SMITH, COFOUNDER AND CEO, ROCKETSHIP PUBLIC SCHOOLS

Get the heck out of the way!

The COVID-19 pandemic has presented immense challenges in many areas of life, but probably none more complex or with higher stakes than schools. I talked with Preston Smith, cofounder and CEO of Rocketship Public Schools, an education organization that operates twenty charter schools in four states, serving approximately ten thousand students. I wanted to see how he and Rocketship were navigating this crisis.

A Complex Puzzle

From the onset of the pandemic, school leaders faced immense pressure to remain open against a backdrop of uncertainty about how the virus spreads, its effects on children, and teacher concerns about their own health. "Many of our kids spend the majority of the day at school," Preston says, "starting at 6:30 or 7 a.m. when they arrive for breakfast and ending as late as 7 p.m. for after-school programming. If we closed, how were we going to take care of our kids and families?"

With school closure a possibility, schools had to figure out how to deliver remote learning and supports while dealing with the very real problem of a lack of technology and Internet access in many households. Then they had to plan how to reopen safely given the almost daily changing guidance. "We had to figure out closure, budget implications, then how to safely open. We had to follow the science, get the PPE, get the filtration, reduce class sizes, and deal with space constraints. Given social distancing guidelines we are only able to serve 50 percent of our kids in person, and we had to figure out what it would look like when half the kids are at home and half are at school. And we had to figure this out in four different states. How do we navigate all this and make it sustainable for teachers?" Schools basically had to come up with a totally new model of education in less than six months.

In addition, they had the challenges of helping kids with severe learning needs or tough home situations, households without Wi-Fi, or situations where mom and dad worked and the kids had to care for younger siblings while also attending classes. "It's a really complex puzzle which at the core of it someone could die. You can't get rid of that risk. Trying to figure this out was massive." So how did they approach it?

Getting Back to Purpose

The very first thing they did was get back to their purpose, the essence of who they are and why they exist. "For us it's about community, joy, and our culture. That's the ethos of our schools. And keeping our kids and staff safe is at its core my responsibility as a leader," Preston shares. "It's not about sending work home. We can figure out the work, but we need to obsess about how we transport our culture to kids at home. It goes back to having a deep understanding of the value we bring."

With that deep understanding, Preston used the following as Rocketship's guiding light: "How are our kids doing? How are our staff doing? And then from there let's build to make it a meaningful instructional learning experience."

"We are at war"—Shift Structure and Operating Principles to Meet the Moment

In a high-stakes crisis situation, recognizing and responding to the crisis as early as possible can be the difference between success and failure. A month before schools were closed, Preston told his team that they were going to shut down. He was met with doubt. "Some people said to me that this was just like the flu and that I was overreacting," Preston recalls. This was a rare time he pulled the CEO card. "Great," he responded, "I'm being crazy. Still do it. Go get ready. Come back to me with a plan."

As part of this plan Preston made a few important moves to navigate the new reality. First, he assessed whether Rocketship was structurally set up for the situation. "We determined that we needed to speed up our move to regionalize our operations, since things were so specific to the particular city or county our schools are in. So we hyper-regionalized and created a single point of contact in each region. I haven't been on a plane since March."

Second, Preston shifted some of his key leadership operating principles. "Typically my approach to leadership is consensus based," he explains, "but what became clear was that we needed to make some quick pivots, and I had to reach into layers of the organization that I don't usually direct. I didn't have time to get consensus. I just needed my team to trust me."

In order to help with this shift, Preston cites the value of being transparent about it. "I told my team, 'We are at war. I am going to be operating differently. This is going to feel uncomfortable for you at times. I need about four to six weeks of massive trust.' Naming it and giving my team a reference point was important."

Third, in crisis, communication and coordination needs to increase. Six weeks before school closures, Rocketship set up a COVID task force that reached beyond the senior leadership team. "Their job was to go get all the data, monitor the situation, and stay up-to-date on the guidance," Preston explains. He also implemented more frequent communication to the board, increased the cadence of staff meetings, spent more time in his one-on-one meetings with team members, and began regular parent surveys. "You've got to check in."

Lastly, as a leader you have to walk the walk and show the courage and vulnerability you expect from your people and help bring them through the trauma and loss they experience. The week before Rocketship closed and went remote, someone in their shared office space tested positive for COVID. Preston recalls, "I felt I needed to go into the office. If I'm asking my team to be there and our teachers to be at school, I need to be there. But deep down I didn't really want to be there."

"It's been trauma on top of trauma," Preston continues. "We've had more kids pass away since March than in our history. We've had staff members who've lost family members. It's so much stuff people are dealing with." Preston's personal experience of loss has allowed him to make sure Rocketship was prepared for this. When he founded his first school a teacher died. "It's really hard. When it's our families, that's brutal, especially when they lose a child. I made sure we had a plan for when people die or we lose somebody, so that if it happens we're ready. We lost my sister seventeen years ago, and I've seen what it does to families," he shared. "You can't say anything right. You try to be there and love them and keep checking in. So how do we continue to show up and check in? We have to help people deal with the trauma of the crisis. We need to go back to operating as normally as we can. The bombing is over, yes we are at war, we have to go into the bunker at night. But during the day we have to go outside and start rebuilding. We need to create normalcy, so people can think longer term."

Of his own self-care Preston says, "I had built rituals and processes to manage myself, and what I failed to recognize is they all went away in COVID. There's no more date night; I didn't play basketball every Saturday; there was no more alone time for me. I'm not managing myself. I need to rebuild those rituals in COVID. I'm sitting too long. So I'm going to make a Zoom call, a phone call, and go out and walk; I'm going to play tennis instead of basketball. Many of us haven't done that. How do we help people build those structures, so coming out of COVID they are still well?"

Use Vision to Keep Looking Forward

Vision has been an important tool in his approach to managing through this crisis. Preston fast-forwarded to the end of the crisis and envisioned what he wanted people to say about how

Rocketship responded. "They were there; they cared for us. I want everyone to know that the most important thing is to keep you alive and safe. The other stuff is going to be messy, and I'm going to apologize in advance, but as an organization that's our priority."

Preston and his team have also been looking for the silver lining in the pandemic. "Great organizations look for the opportunities and go after them," he says, "so we've started sharing more and thinking about how to better share our model." They have also started doing more scenario planning to ensure readiness for potential crises in the future.

It's All about Your Team
The final thing that stood out in my interview with Preston was the last thing he said about how to successfully navigate crisis. He did not make it about himself. Instead he praised his people. He talked about surrounding himself with really smart people and how Rocketship has done a great job of hiring people aligned with its mission, which reaped massive rewards during this period. "There are incredible people throughout Rocketship," he says, "and part of working in schools is the really committed and incredible people. You just have to get the heck out of the way and let them do what they love and are so great at."

Just as I was completing this book, the world changed suddenly, and it felt necessary to reflect on the COVID-19 outbreak and how a new set of realities create opportunities to examine the concepts and stories I've presented. (As I write this now we are in the midst of a mandatory three-week shelter-at-home order.) Our lives have changed drastically, and we are uncertain how bad things will be and for how long. So, what becomes of purpose, values, vision in times of crisis? As I continue to work with clients via phone and video to help them successfully navigate this new reality here is what is emerging.

PEACETIME VS. WARTIME

Former founder, CEO, and current venture investor Ben Horowitz distinguishes between leadership in peacetime and in wartime and the importance of knowing which you are in.

In a crisis, some will turn inward, pull their heads in like turtles and wait until the crisis is over, so they can go back to normal. They send silly emails and binge-watch movies. For others, crisis brings out their most greedy and base side, like those who stockpile hand sanitizer and sell it to make money. However, others are able to navigate crises more effectively, pinpoint areas of growth, discover new opportunities, and emerge stronger than before. For these people, when the status quo doesn't apply anymore, purpose, values, and vision, along with the peak performance tactics outlined in this book become more important than ever. Here are a few key points to think about as we all navigate this new reality and the inevitable crises to come.

Reaffirm Purpose

Remember, purpose is what is most meaningful to us when we are being our best self. Crisis can easily disconnect us from our best self as fear takes over. And while our purpose doesn't change, we need to figure out how we can best express it in the current context and within the constraints we now face. If you are no longer able to express your purpose the way you have been, you must find some new ways to do so. Staying on-purpose will continue to ground you and ensure your actions are consistent with what matters most deeply to you.

Shift Values

Our values can and most likely will change in times of crisis. An example of this would be for a leader, team, or company with a value of being collaborative in "peacetime" shifting their value to being more directive and less inclusive in order to make faster decisions in "wartime." Ask yourself, "What beliefs that guide behaviors are most critical to successfully navigate the current reality?" Choose the four most important as your core "wartime" values. These will enable you to make decisions without having to try to figure out your operating principles every time you must act. And going through this exercise will prevent you from any cognitive dissonance between your "peacetime" values and what is called for now to survive and thrive.

Get Out of the Trenches with Vision

Revisiting your vision in times of crisis can offer some relief from the day-to-day pressures you face by allowing you to spend some time zooming out your focus and spending your time in the future, when hopefully peace has been restored. Your vision may need some adjustment if you believe the new reality is more than just a temporary disruption. Predict what may be different in the future than you had assumed pre-crisis and identify any new opportunities for yourself or your company that you can begin to position yourself for now.

Know When It's "Peacetime" and Know When It's "Wartime"

It's important that you know which world you're in, "peacetime" or "wartime," and make the mental shift to that reality. If you apply the wrong lens to the situation you are in, you will struggle to thrive as you'll have difficulty being on-purpose and using values that aren't built for the current context. And if you don't revise your vision you may be heading to a world that doesn't exist anymore. Later, I offer you a list of questions to help ensure you are making this shift adequately.

I hope we can all use purpose, values, and vision to find a new level of performance during this critical time in our world, one in which we can achieve our goals individually, but also with a focus on solving the problems we face for the sake of our children and their children. They need us to be our best more than ever.

YOUR TURN—PEAK PERFORMANCE IN CRISIS

Use these questions to make sure you are adequately navigating the challenges you are now facing.

What's my purpose and how can I best express it given this new reality?

What has this situation clarified as essential in my life?

What core values will best serve me during this time?

Has this crisis clarified anything new for me that changes my vision?

How do I need to modify goals I've already set for myself and what new goals do I want to set taking this new reality into account?

What areas is this crisis showing me I need to strengthen and develop in my life, family, or business?

What new behaviors, activities, or ways of being do I want to keep once the crisis subsides?

CHAPTER TEN

A Message from the Governor on Conscious Completion

MICHAEL DUKAKIS, FORMER GOVERNOR OF MASSACHUSETTS AND PRESIDENTIAL CANDIDATE

Knowing that endings are merely new beginnings

With every ending comes a new beginning. This is something that was highlighted for me when I interviewed the former presidential candidate Michael Dukakis. Michael Dukakis got involved in politics as much out of anger as anything else. "I grew up in an era when the United States was racist and anti-Semitic. In 1954, Washington was as segregated as Johannesburg, South Africa. Washington schools were segregated by race by an act of Congress. Black folks couldn't eat at restaurants. They had just stopped having to go to the back of the bus—in DC! What we call the capital of the free world."

It wasn't until Senator Joe McCarthy began making accusations about people's loyalty to the United States in the early 1950s that Dukakis's interest in politics turned into action. While he was still in college, he began volunteering on local campaigns to gain experience. The first office he ever ran for was with the local Redevelopment Authority of Brookline, Massachusetts, while he was attending law school. He lost by 120 votes, but this near miss only motivated him further. The following year he ran for town meeting member, and this time he won. Two years later, in 1962, he ran for and won a seat in the state legislature and went on to serve four terms in the Massachusetts House of Representatives. In 1974, Dukakis was elected governor of Massachusetts, where he served three terms. And in 1988, he became the Democratic presidential nominee.

Every time he ran for office, his high school French teacher would send him $10 to help fund his campaign. When she passed away, Dukakis received a letter saying that she had left him $1,000 with the hope that he would use it to run for the presidency. At that time, he was running for his third term as governor and hadn't considered running for president. "That became the first contribution to my presidential campaign."

The 1988 presidential race pitted Dukakis against George H. W. Bush. The Bush campaign accused Dukakis of being soft on crime, weak on foreign policy, and even raised questions about his mental health. But these attacks did not discourage Dukakis. Quite the contrary, they motivated him to work harder to win. "When you see your polling numbers going down, it's not a question of getting deflated, but trying to deal with what you're facing and coming up with some answers." What Dukakis remembers from that time was working to overcome the rough patches he was facing the summer before the election and that they were closing on Bush, but not fast enough.

Despite the nasty campaign tactics employed by the other side and his eventual loss, Dukakis says that running for president was a fantastic experience. In his concession speech, he had a special message for the young people of this country, which still holds to this day: "I hope many of you will go into politics and public service. It's a noble profession." While one might think losing in a landslide in a presidential election would be incredibly difficult to bounce back from, Dukakis returned to his purpose, values, and vision and has worked tirelessly to support the next generation of public servants.

The way we end things matters. It's the difference between stumbling into the next thing frazzled and tired, sure to repeat the same mistakes, or taking the time to reflect on what happened, celebrate the good, assess what could have been better, extract key learnings, and leave behind what will hold you back in the future. In coaching, we call this "conscious completion," a defined time and space to do what we need to do in order to move on.

Conscious completion can be used whenever something important or meaningful in your life is coming to an end. It can help make experiences that aren't particularly important more significant. You can consciously complete with big life changes, such as the end of a relationship, the end of a job, moving to a new city, or anything that you want to get more out of, which could include reading this book. There is no single right way to consciously complete. It could be taking some time to write about your experience. It could be going away for a few days to a quiet place; walking in nature; talking to a friend, therapist, or coach. However you choose to bring closure to something, here are some questions you might want to use in your conscious completion process:

How was this experience for me?

What am I really proud of and grateful for?

What could I have done differently or better?

What are the key learnings I would like to hold on to?

What will not serve me next that I want to let go of?

Spend enough time and thought with these questions, and any others you want to reflect on, until you have a feeling of completion, that you can move on with 100 percent focus to your next endeavor. Because remember, with every ending comes an opportunity for a new beginning.

CONCLUSION

The 30-Day Peak Performance Challenge

I wanted to end my book consciously by providing you with a 30-day plan to help implement the Peak Performance Formula in your own life. Now that you have completed this book and homed in on your purpose, gotten clear on your values and the gaps in how you're living them, created a compelling vision for yourself and learned the tools and techniques of sustained peak performance, you have everything you need to step into the realm of breakthrough improvement. Like anything else in life, you only get out what you put in. So I've designed a 30-day program for you that will help you implement the tools and techniques in this book and begin making them habits. There will be setbacks. This is not easy. But as long as you remember that setbacks are the best learning opportunities, you will prevail.

Week 1: Vision and Goals

We start our 30-day program with the end in mind. This will make sure that you spend the next month focused on the right things.

Day 1: Vision. Complete either the Time Machine or the Three- to Six-Month Vision exercise provided at the end of Chapter Four on vision and goals. Get as clear and detailed as you can on what you'd like the future to look like.

Day 2: Goal-Setting. Select one aspect of your vision that you would like to spend the next twenty-nine days focused on making breakthrough improvement or progress. It might be an area related to your health, relationships, career, financial situation, personal growth, or a passion project or any other area of your life that is important to you right now. Once you choose an area to focus on, it's time to set your goal (i.e., the outcome you want to see) at the end of the 30-day challenge. Use the Goal-Setting process for this provided in the vision and goal-setting chapter of the book. When you're done, you should have a set of three to five objectives for your goal and three to five Key Results that ensure that you will achieve each objective. You can look at the first week as foundation-building, the second week as ramping up, the third week as priming, and the fourth week as performing. So if your goal is to play and perform well in a competitive tennis match, the match should happen during the last week of the challenge. Each week you will score your Key Results to keep you on track and course correct where needed.

Day 3: Make Yourself Fail-Proof. So that this challenge doesn't become yet another stressful obligation, use the reframing technique I provide to make yourself fail-proof. Write down how this next twenty-seven days will be about your own growth, the impact you hope to make on yourself and the world, the relationships you will cultivate as you pursue your goal, and how you will find enjoyment in the process. By grounding in this perspective you will increase your odds of success.

Day 4: Build Your Team. Now that you are clear on your vision and goals, and you've framed this challenge so that you cannot fail, it's time to put together the supports that will help you stay the course and succeed. Refer to Chapter Five, which discusses the benefits of building a support team. List who you need to help you and what help you need from them. Choose someone to share your goal, Objectives, and Key Results with and ask them to provide daily or weekly accountability for you. Is there a subject matter expert who can accelerate your progress in the area you are focusing on? Now would be a good time to seek him or her out and enlist their support toward achieving your goal.

Day 5–6: Do the Work Like a Peak Performer exercise. Over these next two days get to work on accomplishing your Key Results. Stay focused on them and don't get distracted by other shiny objects. Remember your Key Results are the highest leverage, highest priority action items that will get you to achieve your Objectives. Use deliberate practice, periods of no more than two hours of single focus on those activities with seven- to twenty-minute breaks in between to ensure your highest productivity. At the end of Day 6, score your Key Results and share them with your designated accountability person to see where you made good progress and where you need to pick up the pace. Check in with your team about the week and any adjustments for next week.

Day 7: Recover Like a Peak Performer. You've done six days of great effort. It's time to rest and recover. Take today off from pursuing your goal. Do things that have nothing to do with your goal, that are relaxing, restorative, and fun. Take a nap, get extra sleep.

Week 2: Purpose and Values

Week 1 ensured that we identified the right thing to focus on. Week 2 supercharges your efforts by enlisting your purpose in your cause and articulating a set of values specifically designed to ensure you meet your goals.

Day 8: Purpose Statement. If you haven't done so already, using the purpose statement exercise in Chapter Two, come up with a good enough draft of your purpose statement. Make sure it motivates you to achieve the 30-day goal you set for yourself, especially the parts that aren't inherently fun or exciting to you. Invoke your purpose statement first thing each morning before getting out of bed. Write down and post your purpose statement in various places where you will see it when you are working toward your 30-day challenge goal. When feeling a lack of motivation to do the work involved in your plan, call on your purpose to get you reengaged.

Day 9: Values. Using the values exercise (Chapter Three) make a list of all the values (phrased as behaviors) that will lead you to meeting your goal. Circle the four most important to guide you over the next twenty-one days. These are your 30-Day Challenge core values. Post them in a few places where you will see them throughout the day. When faced with a tough choice or decision related to the challenge, use the values to guide you.

Day 10: Bring Your Whole Self. Now that we've got the powerful tools of purpose and values supercharging us toward breakthrough progress, let's make sure we are using all of ourselves to achieve our goals. We never want to lift a heavy weight using only our arms. We're not as strong that way. We want to use everything we have. Complete the Whole Self activity in the Becoming a Peak Performer chapter to identify aspects of yourself that have gone dormant and answer the following question: How could I use those aspects of myself to more effectively achieve my 30-Day peak performance goal?

Days 11–13: Do the Work Like a Peak Performer. Over these next three days focus on accomplishing your Key Results. Keep invoking your purpose and using your values to guide you. Stay focused and don't get distracted by shiny objects. Use deliberate practice, periods of no more than two hours of single focus on those activities with seven-to-twenty-minute breaks to ensure your highest productivity. At the end of Day 13, score your Key Results and share them with your designated accountability coach to see where you made good progress and where you need to pick up the pace. Check in with your team about the week and any adjustments for next week. You are about halfway through the challenge. Keep up the great work!

Day 14: Recover Like a Peak Performer. You've completed thirteen days of great effort. It's time to rest and recover. Take today off from pursuing your goal. Do things that have nothing to do with your goal that are relaxing, restorative, and fun. Take a nap, get extra sleep.

Week 3: Become a Peak Performer

Weeks 1 and 2 got the pillars of the Peak Performance Formula solidly in place. You are utilizing purpose, values, and vision to move you powerfully toward your goal. This week you will be adding the adjunctive tools and techniques that will elevate you to true peak performer status.

Day 15: The Physical. You are halfway through the challenge you set for yourself and have been harnessing all your energy toward your goal. You may be feeling tired from the level of focus and effort you've been giving. Remember, a hallmark of breakthrough performance is our ability to sustain that focus and effort over time, day in and day out. Today we will pay special attention to how you are managing and maximizing your energy. Double down on single tasking (put that phone away), adjust the time of day you are working on your challenge for when you are most alert and focused, and for the remainder of the challenge choose one decision you can automate to conserve your mental energy (e.g., wear the same outfit for the next fifteen days, eat the same thing for lunch, etc.). We've been building in breaks throughout the day as well as recovery days. Check in with yourself to see if those are enough or if you need more recovery. And of course make sure you are getting adequate sleep and taking naps where needed. These adjustments should give you the energy you need to push through to the end.

Day 16: Technical. Let's make sure you're honing whatever technical skill is involved in achieving your goal. Is there a set of chords you need to master on your guitar, is there a shot you need to improve on the tennis court, is getting better at speaking in public required? We've already built deliberate practice into your plan. Let's make sure you have designed your plan well by reviewing it to see if the Key Results you initially set will lead you to achieve your goal. Are they too easy or too hard? They should be stretching you just enough. If they are not, revise them. Once you're sure you've got the right plan in place, focus on repetition. Finally, get yourself some feedback to see how you're doing. Perhaps this is from someone on the team you assembled in the first week of the challenge. Or maybe it is video recording yourself to pick up the nuances of your technique that need adjusting.

Day 17: Mental. Today we will address the mental game of performance. Two days ago we tended to our physical energy, and yesterday we made sure to pay extra attention to the technical aspects our goal requires. Today and into next week, you will work to make sure your mind is helping you as opposed to impeding you in achieving your goal. We will start this process with some mindfulness practice to quiet the noise in our heads and strengthen our focus. Starting today find eight minutes to sit quietly with your spine straight, observing the breath coming in and out of your nose. When your mind wanders, notice it and bring your attention back to your breath. Do this every day for the remainder of the challenge, striving to get up to twenty minutes (the minimum most effective dose) per day.

Days 18–20: Do the Work Like a Peak Performer. Over these next three days focus on accomplishing your Key Results. Keep invoking your purpose and using your values to guide you. Stay focused and don't get distracted by shiny objects. Use deliberate practice, periods of no more than two hours of single focus on those activities with seven- to twenty-minute breaks in between to ensure your highest productivity. And make sure these periods are aligned to the time of day you are most alert and focused. At the end of Day 20, score your Key Results and share them with your designated accountability person to see where you made good progress and where you need to pick up the pace. Check in with your team about the week and any adjustments for next week.

Find eight to twenty minutes to practice mindfulness meditation each day. You are more than halfway through the challenge. Keep up the great work!

Day 21: Recover Like a Peak Performer. You've done twenty days of great effort. It's time to rest and recover. Take today off from pursuing your goal. Do things that have nothing to do with your goal that are relaxing, restorative, and fun. Take a nap, get extra sleep, and continue your mindfulness meditation practice.

Week 4: The Peak Performance Mindset

You are in your final week of the 30-day Challenge. In this final push we want to make sure you are continuing to hone the mental skills needed to achieve sustained high performance. By this time you should be nearing the completion of your goal, which involves performing at levels you haven't before. It's time for your performance breakthrough. Let's get to work.

Day 22: Tame the Imposter. By this point, if not earlier, you may have started to hear some voices of doubt about whether or not you are up to this challenge. This is your imposter syndrome rearing its ugly head. If you haven't already, complete the Transforming Limiting Beliefs exercise in the Becoming a Peak Performer chapter of the book. Use the mantra you come up with at the end of the exercise to help you push through those moments of doubt that slow you down and derail you from achieving your goals. These voices of self-doubt will get especially loud when things aren't going well or are getting challenging. Don't give in. You've got this.

Day 23: Manage Your Stress. As we discussed earlier in the book, stress is a natural part of performance. We need to be able to manage it. You already have a number of stress-reduction techniques that work for you. Write them down and more actively deploy them starting today.

Rather than suffering, remember that the goal you have set and the challenges associated with it are exciting and meaningful. Employ at least one strategy from the section on managing stress (get a massage, take a bath, do the Three Good Things activity, start 4-7-8 breathing, etc.) and notice its impact. Use that technique and the others each day from now until the end of the challenge.

Day 24: Overcome Fear and Performance Anxiety. We know that when we're stretching ourselves to new limits and doing something we haven't done before, fear of the unknown and getting nervous when it's time to perform can debilitate us. Today, we will use the strategies to help us bring these factors into more manageable range. Review the section on fear and performance anxiety (Chapter Five) and implement as many of the strategies as you can today and each day moving forward. For example, if your goal is to give an amazing presentation at work, spend time in the room where you will be presenting. If your goal is to run a longer distance than you've ever run before, do a run where you practice focusing on only the next mile, not the many miles after that. Close your eyes while you're practicing (unless it would be dangerous to do so) to get the feeling of it in your body. Implementing these strategies each day from now until the end of the challenge will ensure you are performance-ready.

Day 25–27: Do the Work Like a Peak Performer. Over these next three days, make a final push to accomplish your Key Results. The end is in sight. Keep invoking your purpose and using your values to guide you. Stay focused and don't get distracted by shiny objects. Use your deliberate practice, periods of no more than two hours of single focus on those activities with seven- to twenty-minute breaks in between to ensure your highest productivity. And make sure these periods are aligned to the time of day you are most alert and focused. At the end of Day 27, score your Key Results and share them with your designated accountability person to see where you made good progress. Check in with your team about the week and any final push you can make on your final day. Find eight to twenty minutes to practice mindfulness meditation each day. Keep the imposter at bay and your nervous system calm. You're almost there!

Day 28: Recover Like a Peak Performer. You've finished twenty-seven days of great effort. Even though you're close to the end, it's still time to rest and recover. You're playing the long game of sustained high performance. Take today off from pursuing your goal. Do things that have nothing to do with your goal that are relaxing, restorative, and fun. Take a nap, get extra sleep, and continue your mindfulness meditation practice.

Day 29: Final Push! This is your last day. Make a final push in your highest leverage area. What is one thing you can do that will give you the greatest progress toward your goal? Run as hard as you can. Invoke your purpose today, and let that carry you home.

Day 30: Conscious Completion. Congratulations! You've completed your 30-Day Peak Performance Challenge. It's time to take stock. Refer back to the section on conscious completion (Chapter Ten) and use the prompts provided there to close out these past thirty days. End this process for yourself by saying, "I am complete." And you are.

If this felt like a lot that's because it was. Performing at your highest level is hard and takes this kind of commitment. Typically, you'll have a little more breathing room as your goals will be longer term and you won't need to condense the Peak Performance Formula into such a tight time frame. This challenge was not just about accomplishing breakthrough performance and achieving your goal. It was just as much about learning how to apply the concepts and techniques of the Peak Performance Formula in real life and building the muscles to use them in whatever endeavor you wish to realize your potential.

ACKNOWLEDGMENTS

I believe that everyone has at least one book to give the world, something only they could create based on their unique life experience. We all have a story to tell. While I am only one author, many people made it possible, and I want to thank them here.

First, to all my teachers (even the one who told me my *Stuart Little* book report was too long), thank you for stoking my curiosity and making me always want to learn more. To Jim Farganis, my college advisor who showed me what true intellectual rigor was: the highest standards of thinking combined with compassion when trying to figure difficult things out. To my Buddhist teachers, thank you for showing me an alternative way to understand my mind and emotions and gain more peace in this chaotic world. Thanh Mai, you showed me what purpose looks like in action; and the monks at Tu Hieu monastery (Thich Nhat Hanh's home before his exile), you showed me how to get over myself (I still chuckle when I imagine myself doing Kung Fu with the novice monks). To my teachers and supervisors in psychoanalytic training, especially Alan Dolber, Marc Sholes, and Pam Feldman, thank you for teaching me, with rigor and kindness, this most wonderful method for realizing potential. And thank you to my coaching trainers at CTI, with special thanks to Ken Mosseman, who was my first coach, and Graham Coppin, who I will assert, along with Ken, are the best coaching teachers out there.

I'd like to thank my therapy and coaching clients, who have been the catalyst for much of the contents in the book. You are the smartest, most committed, and most passionate people I know, and it's been an honor helping you make your visions a reality, as messy as it can be at times. And a special thanks to Avidan Ross, founding partner at Root Ventures, for effectively getting me started as a "silicon valley" coach. I still remember the conversation we had that day, strolling around downtown Manhattan, that solidified for me my method of peak performance coaching. Thank you for believing in me and making those first introductions.

Thank you to these peak performers for sharing your stories to help us live more successful and fulfilling lives: Jim Courier, Governor Michael Dukakis, Ethan Zohn, Professor Ronald Heifetz, Dick Hoyt, Max Erdstein, Nancy Baker, Nancy Meyers Coolidge, Martin Strel, Jack Heath, Garrett Dutton, Vicki Knott, Preston Smith, Brent Baker, Charlie Chen, Lhadon Tethong, and Suraya Sadeed. You are an inspiration.

Angela Engel and her team at the Collective Book Studio gave my writing what it needed to go from an interesting jumble of ideas to a cohesive and well-formed book. In particular, Lee Bruno, your passionate editorial guidance was just what I needed and more than I could have hoped for. Even through a gnarly bike injury, you never relented as my number-one champion. And to Dean Burrell, who expertly guided the manuscript to production. The seeming effortlessness that Dean exudes is a true mark of mastery.

In the book I talk about assembling a team, as elite athletes do, to help you reach your goals. I'm indebted to my team, who helps make everything in my life work: Dr. Ivan Barron, my good friend, who is always up for an adventure with me; Jay Mercado, my personal trainer, who makes sure I have the strength and energy to do everything; my tennis coach, Milan, for giving me the confidence to compete again; and to AR, for so lovingly caring for our children so I can work without worry or distraction.

And last but not least, thank you to my family, my loving wife, Deborah, and three beautiful children—Satya, Sequoia, and Mischa—who have given my life purpose beyond anything I ever imagined while also pushing me to new levels of peak performance needed to keep up with you. I'm not sure how, but somehow I managed to finish this book during the COVID-19 pandemic with a newborn baby. To me this is further validation that with a grounding purpose, guiding values, and clear vision and the right structures in place anything is attainable. I am living proof.